My First Year as a Journalist

MY FIRST YEAR
AS A
JOURNALIST

REAL-WORLD
STORIES
FROM
AMERICA'S NEWSPAPER AND
MAGAZINE JOURNALISTS

Edited By

DIANNE SELDITCH

WALKER AND COMPANY
NEW YORK

First published in the United States of America in 1995 by Walker Publishing Company, Inc.

Published simultaneously in Canada by Thomas Allen & Son Canada, Limited, Markham, Ontario

Library of Congress Cataloging-in-Publication Data
My first year as a journalist : real-world stories from America's newspaper and magazine journalists / edited by Dianne Selditch.
p.   cm.—(First year career series)
Includes index.
ISBN 0-8027-1295-9 (hardcover).—ISBN 0-8027-7426-1 (pbk.)
1. Journalism—United States—Anecdotes.   2. Reporters and reporting—United States—Anecdotes.   I. Selditch, Dianne.
II. Series.
PN4797.M89   1995
071'.3—dc20   94-30748
CIP

Book design by Glen M. Edelstein

Printed in the United States of America

2   4   6   8   10   9   7   5   3   1

To Jay

Contents

FOREWORD   *Charles R. Eisendrath*   ix

ACKNOWLEDGMENTS   xiii

INTRODUCTION   *Dianne Selditch*   xv

1. I Almost Got Fired   *Beth Cooney*   1

2. A Ballet of Chaos   *Timothy McDarrah*   9

3. An Eye on History   *Helen Thomas*   20

4. Ask, and Ask Again   *Goldie Blumenstyk*   27

5. Detail! Detail! Detail!   *Mary Schmich*   36

6. The Cop Beat   *Wayne Dawkins*   44

7. Rhythm and Dues   *Anne Groer*   53

8. Clarity Above All   *Craig Neff*   62

9. You'll Eventually Get a Break   *Graham Hovey*   72

10. No Safety Net, No Shortcuts   *Betsy Carter*   81

11. The Case of the Missing Lids   *Pam Luecke*   88

12. Trust Your Instincts   *Mireya Navarro*   96

13. Stabbings and Sacred Cows   *Stephen L. Petranek*   105

14. Ducks Versus Geese   *Dave Barry*   115

15. A Special License   *George Judson*   121

16. A Foot in the Door   *Ellie McGrath*   131

17. Gotta Get the Story   *Jeff Zaslow*   138

18. Michael and Me   *L. Carol Ritchie*   146

19. A Good Story Stays with You   *Michael Agovino*   154

20. From Fiction to Fact   *Melinda Lewis-Matravers*   161

21. *Life* in the Big Time   *Frances Glennon*   169

22. The Last Page   *Mitch Gerber*   177

INDEX   183

Foreword

More than most lines of work, reporting is a street-corner trade. By that I mean that you are more likely to get into it because of what somebody needs right then than by dint of native brilliance, advanced degrees, or where you come from. Metaphorically speaking (and maybe metaphysically, too), you are simply on the right corner when some editor needs somebody just like you, or close enough so you'll do.

True, pull and/or a master's degree can help. But reporting isn't like most other activities. It can't be faked. Get it wrong, and someone's calling on the phone or writing a letter to the editor. "It," of course, can be anything. Count the facts in a newspaper story sometime. There are lots of them, and each is an "it." Even if someone gets you a reporting job, you are unlikely to keep it beyond the tryout period if you can't get it quick, get it right, and, most important, get it the way your editor thinks it should be got.

If this sounds to you random, normative, and altogether unlike social science—where universities sometimes house journalism departments, in total disregard of what journalism is, which is not particularly social and assuredly not science—well then, you might make a fair reporter. Journalism is just as random, normative, and unlike academia as it's possible to be. Rather like human existence itself, which is why it offers more unpredictable interest than any other profession. Anyone in journalism will tell you that the first year was the most important. This book goes farther in telling you why. It is a sort of campfire. Listen up. The elders are telling their stories.

The great thing about campfire stories is how little they seem like education, although that's exactly what they are. Nobody's telling you what to do, merely what they did. Although the delineations differ and the colors vary (and what colors!), certain constants emerge as the earth and sky of journalistic personalities. Curiosity. A willingness and maybe even an eagerness to go anywhere to do anything. A lot of energy. Intolerance of hypocrisy. A way with language, words, and people. The presence of a mentor.

The mentors deserve special consideration. As this book goes to press, the determining watchwords in the nation's newsrooms are "sensitivity" and "comfort," meaning that journalists, like others, should be solicitous of others' feelings so that nobody feels offended. The mentors who played such important roles in these first years are anything but sensitive. Those they instruct are anything but comfortable. Are they bad people? Atavisms? Hardly. They simply express the inherited wisdom of the profession: "Get it right, first. We'll discuss everything else after deadline." One of the many interesting aspects of this book is the contrast it draws between what leading journalists remember about their best teachers and mentors and the values strived for today.

For the last seven years, I have run a fellowship program at the University of Michigan that brings journalists back to formal studies at a point somewhere near the middle of their careers.

Competition is tough: Only one in ten applicants is accepted, which of course leads to the considerable prestige enjoyed by those who make it. The goal is to improve the quality of news available to the American public by helping some of the most talented journalists reach peak performance at a speed and level faster and higher than would be possible otherwise.

To the fellows, of course, it means something less lofty but one hell of a lot more immediate: an academic year off at someone else's expense, and a chance to learn things that there somehow hasn't been time for. That happens, of course, but the real importance is quite different.

In the break from newsroom demands, which over time can blunt enthusiasm for even the most interesting and important events, something happens to journalism fellows. I begin to see it in the spring, after they've been at the university for six months or so. It doesn't seem to matter whether they've been studying international economics or the importance of women in Victorian novels. A certain infectiousness comes back into their pleasure in the new, although, as grown-up professionals in their thirties and forties, they often try to disguise it.

It's pretty clear what has happened. They have returned to the campfire. They have gotten back in touch with their own first years, the ones that they describe in very much the terms you're about to read.

—Charles R. Eisendrath,
director, Michigan Journalism
Fellows, University of Michigan

Acknowledgments

A journalist never knows what a phone call will bring. One afternoon an editor at Walker and Company left a message on my
telephone answering machine suggesting that we work together on
a project. The call, from Mary Kennan Herbert, led to this collection, and I thank her and Sarah Collins. Their counsel has been
invaluable.

The assignment gave me a wonderful excuse to interview former colleagues as well as writers and editors I had never met. I
owe each of them a special thanks for taking time from their
deadlines to help me meet mine. I am particularly grateful to Graham Hovey and his wife, Mary Jean, for their unceasing faith and
encouragement.

I thank my parents, Nathan and Beatrice, and my sister, Robin,
for their belief in me.

And I am most grateful to my husband and pal, Jay Zelermyer,
whose emotional surefootedness and technical support kept this
project moving in the right direction.

Introduction

Helen Thomas, the White House correspondent who is in her fifth decade with United Press International, began her career as a copyboy, fetching coffee and ripping wire stories dispatched from the battlefields of World War II. Pam Luecke, a Pulitzer Prize–winning editor, wrote wedding announcements. Betsy Carter, who works in New York City as editor-in-chief of *New Woman*, covered sewers for a trade newsletter, and Dave Barry, award-winning humor columnist, finally learned to ask his sources the intimate question: how to spell their names. These are among the first-year experiences of the writers and editors you will meet in this collection of first-person accounts by men and women who have made careers in newspapers and magazines.

For journalists such as Graham Hovey, a former war correspondent and editorial writer at *The New York Times*, that first job coincided with the end of the Depression and the momentous events leading to World War II. For others coming of age within the past three decades, the benchmark is pre- or post-Watergate, when two reporters at *The Washington Post* inadvertently steered so many college graduates into journalism they had to compete with one another for dwindling magazine and newspaper jobs.

Listening to their voices, and the common experiences that resonate among the chapters, you will hear what motivated these career writers and editors to go into journalism, what they learned as novices, and how their attitudes have changed over the years. You may also discover something new about the profession. I certainly did. The most surprising outcome of this volume is that it became a crash course on becoming a journalist: from Beth Cooney, that the work is rarely, if ever, nine-to-five; from Goldie Blumenstyk, that questions must be asked, and asked again; from Michael Agovino, that you'll get impatient waiting for your break; and from Ellie McGrath and L. Carol Ritchie, that an imperfect first job can help you define what you really want.

Within each chapter are valuable insights gained while handling first assignments or observing seasoned colleagues. Anne Groer still hears the voice of a veteran reporter who dictated a riot story while hiding under a table at a Newark, New Jersey, beauty parlor. Mary Schmich was mentored in California by an editor who demanded that reporters be able to recite from the writers' bible, *The Elements of Style* by William Strunk Jr. and E. B. White. Mitch Gerber learned from one whose mantra was to read to the end because you never know what you'll find. Frances Glennon trained her eye alongside an editor who, though occasionally inarticulate, was a master at selecting photographs. Timothy McDarrah was constantly amazed that the same editors who sit around talking sports could orchestrate coverage of the big story and rarely miss a beat.

In that crucial first year, these journalists quickly recognized that they work in a solitary business that relies on independent judgment and seat-of-the-pants intuition. You're constantly asked to make ethical calls, says Wayne Dawkins. Stephen Petranek abandoned his post at the police station without informing his editors and ran several city blocks to the scene of a stabbing. Jeff Zaslow bent at the grave of a young girl, copying the names of people who had sent flowers to identify potential interviewees. Mireya Navarro deliberately locked herself out of her car. They wanted to get the story. The technology used to transmit copy may be different for today's first-year journalist but not the grit required to produce it.

Assaulted by a constant stream of words and actions, writers and editors must harness disparate details into so many inches of copy. Each decision filters the story for the reader. Whether covering a track-and-field event, a single speech, or analyzing a series of conflicting interviews, reporters first ask themselves, "What's important? What's different? What's of interest to the reader? What do I understand sufficiently to explain?" An editor then has the job of reading for clarity and cohesiveness, for missing information, for grammar and spelling, and for the sensibility that a particular editor brings to a piece. One decides whether to change a word in the text, what to emphasize in a headline, which illustration or photograph will accompany the piece. Another may select the page on which the article appears, signaling a degree of importance by its placement. Other people will second-guess you, but at the moment of contact with the event or written word, you're alone.

This business of gathering, ordering, writing, rechecking, editing, and publishing information is shaped by so many people it's a wonder the printed word resembles what actually occurred. That's why fact checkers are so important, says Melinda Lewis-Matravers. The entire sequence at newspapers can begin and end within twenty-four hours; with magazines it can take months. In either case, the element of elapsed time between event and publication adds another filter. At best, suggests George Judson, an article is a truthful account of what writers and editors believed on any given day. Errors have consequences. Misinformation, says Craig Neff, can enter the publishing food chain and get reprinted and digested as fact.

This book enjoys no immunity from the imperfections inherent in journalism. The survey is random, unscientific, and demographically incomplete. The chapters are based on taped conversations with writers and editors who relied on their best recollections and boxes of yellowed clips. Graham Hovey's is the one exception; his chapter is excerpted from his unpublished memoirs. Their accounts, though not rewritten by me, were inevitably shaped by my decisions about which details to leave out and what anecdotes to emphasize. The contributors had the opportunity to refine their chapters, which were edited again by my editors. Yet out of this very fallible, human process, certain basic truths about the first year in journalism emerge, their essence intact.

I've been around journalists for twenty years and until I began working on this book still thought I was the only one who got nervous about asking a school board member why she had voted a certain way, or who felt I wasn't a "real reporter" because I had not covered a statehouse. Others in the newsroom seemed so confident, so willing to jump into the fray. But in these pages are admissions from journalists who not only confess to inexplicable errors that still rub—misspelling the name of a person featured in a profile—but also lament gaps in their careers.

I find it fascinating that these men and women came to be reporters and editors for different reasons: a high school byline that branded them as a journalist; an opening on a college paper; a love interest that brought them to a particular town and job; a momentary whim.

I fall into the last category. I was living in central Florida, waiting tables at a roadside steakhouse that played live country music, watching daytime TV broadcasts of John Dean testifying before the Senate Judiciary Committee, and stumped about my true professional calling. (I had retired after two years teaching English, finding it intolerable that I could be found in the same high school classroom, on any given day, at any given time, repeating the same words, "Please sit down and be quiet.") An acquaintance mentioned that the newspaper where he worked was hiring reporters, and I thought, "I like to write; I like to talk to people." I knew nothing about working for daily newspapers, but growing up in Miami I had read *The Miami Herald* every day after school and had written an article or two for my junior high school paper.

The next morning, while I waited to speak with the city editor, a woman walked in, and before she had a chance to put her purse down, the city editor shouted out to her, "Grab your notebook. I want you to get to the Ramada Inn. I need the interview." She had not been in that office for more than two minutes, and as far as I knew, had no idea what she'd be doing that day. I was hooked. I filled out the application, left it on the editor's desk, and drove to a nearby town, where I completed applications at two other newspaper bureaus. *The Orlando Sentinel* suggested that I apply the next day at its main office. I didn't have an appointment, but an hour after arriving I was led upstairs into a huge, carpetless, windowless room with desks arranged in various configurations: Some were L-shaped, others like spokes, still others in rows. I told the editor I wanted to be a reporter. "We're only looking at people with three years' experience," he said. Then he asked if I could type. I had been working as a temp, and my typing speed was fast. They hired me on the spot, as a clerk at $80 a week, to answer phones and take dictation. "Are you sure you don't want to teach? It pays a lot more than journalism," said the managing editor, Ken Michael. No, I said. I was sure.

Newspaper offices were so foreign, I was intrigued by the newness of everything. The newspaper published editions throughout the day, and Ken Michael, who relished the business, savored the cycle of deadlines that energized the newsroom, most notably in late afternoon. Night-shift copy editors appeared at their desks; reporters returned to their typewriters to bang out their stories; and news editors huddled in meetings to decide which stories would appear on the front page. I knew nothing about the jargon or culture of the newsroom but got such a kick out of calling other reporters, especially women, by their last names. I had never referred to a teaching colleague by her last name. I took dictation from funeral directors telephoning "obits" and from reporters "on assignment" who had called "the desk," never an editor, just the desk. I typed on legal-size sheets of newsprint rolled into a manual Royal typewriter, and "slugged" each story by giving it a single-word name typed in the top left-hand corner. Each page was called a "take," and reporters always typed "-30-" at the bottom of the last page to signal the end of the story. To avoid retyping a page, we corrected and revised with thick, soft-lead pencils, inserting and deleting words by using proofreaders' marks. Copy was considered "dirty" if it had too many corrections. If we wanted to reorganize a story without retyping, or needed to move a "graf" from one page to another, we cut the section by ripping it against a "pica pole," a metal ruler that measures inches and picas. We then reattached the cut sections with rubber cement kept in brown jars called glue pots. (This relic is now reincarnated on my personal computer as the icon for "paste.")

We pasted all the takes together into one long sheet, and when it was edited, the copykids rolled the pages and placed them in pneumatic tubes, similar to those found at drive-in bank windows, and dropped them into some dark place that whisked the tubes to the press room on the ground floor. When I left the *Sentinel* thirteen years later (with a year off as a University of Michigan Journalism Fellow) to move north, I had covered most beats, made the transition from hot type to computers, and held several editing positions, including Sunday magazine editor. Like Ken Michael, I was struck by the notion that much of the paper was conceived, produced, and delivered in one day. "You'll get ink in your veins," he warned me that first year. He was right.

More than once in these chapters, you will hear writers and editors say they are still astonished they can earn their living by doing work they love. You knock on a door, someone opens it, you're invited in, and another life plays out before you. As a journalist, the world is yours for the taking, just by asking a question. I'm continually surprised that most people respond. And I am especially grateful to these journalists for answering my questions and for sharing with us their first years in journalism.

1

I Almost Got Fired

 BETH COONEY

The Transcript Telegram had deadlines at nine-thirty in the morning. I had to be in at seven and file my stories by nine, then spend the afternoon reporting for the next day. I often covered night meetings as well. I was exhausted and getting burned out. I started to rebel. Many days I would walk out early, insisting that I was only paid to work forty hours a week and that was all I was going to work. I would finish the story the next morning. It was 1984. I was making $210 a week and thinking, "This isn't as glamorous as I thought it was going to be." I had been working three or four months as the education reporter at this small afternoon newspaper in Holyoke, Massachusetts, when the paper hired a new assistant city editor from a larger paper in Colorado. He was an award-winning education reporter who not only had written all the stories I needed to write but had won awards for them. And here I was, a twenty-one-year-old who didn't know anything about my beat.

I was struggling with my transition from college student to

working person earning a paycheck. And I was still very much into my college lifestyle, going to Cape Cod for weekends and going out with my friends at night. When a major story broke one Friday afternoon, I broke into tears.

"I'm supposed to be at happy hour on the Cape at six," I cried, knowing the Cape was two and half hours away and I'd never get there in time if I covered the story. I was really upset at missing the opportunity to be with my friends.

My editor, the award-winning education reporter, just shook his head and looked at me. From his desk drawer, he pulled out a flask (which I later learned was always empty) and said, without much sympathy, "Have happy hour here. Now get your story done."

Shortly thereafter I was called into his office and told that if I didn't get my act together, I'd be fired. I walked out, went into the bathroom, and threw up. "I'm good," I thought. "He has no right to talk to me that way."

"You are potentially a very good reporter," he had admonished me. "But you're not willing to work as hard as somebody in this business needs to work. You say at the end of eight hours, 'Well, my story's not done, but so what, I'm going home.'" He was right. I had said that, more than once, planning to finish it the next morning before deadline.

"That's not how it works in this business," he had told me. And I hadn't understood. I thought you got paid to work eight hours, and you worked eight hours. I knew that people in journalism worked hard. But I had too many friends in the business world who were working from nine to five and then were free to party, and I was comparing myself to people who were in other businesses and professions.

But I didn't want to lose that job. After the confrontation with my editor, I started to work like a slave. I rarely left the office before six, even though *The Telegram* was an afternoon paper and technically, my day ended around three. I was there day and night, putting in sixty or seventy hours a week. My assignment was to cover the city schools of Holyoke as well as Mount Holyoke College and Smith College. When covering night meetings, reporters were supposed to split their shift and leave the office before noon and return in the evening. Instead, I stayed until midafternoon. I then covered the meeting until it ended, often at eleven at night, and returned at seven the next morning to file fresh copy for that day's edition.

My main competition was a morning daily. Because our stories appeared in the afternoon, and the "news" wasn't necessarily new, a rule at *The Telegram* was that our stories had to be distinctly different from those in the competing paper. We had to have second-day leads.

This was not easy. When the school board passed a resolution on sex education, for example, I started my morning at a local school and ran like a mad dog between seven and eight-thirty looking for teachers, students, or principals who could make the story come alive by commenting on how the board's action affected them. I then had about a half hour left to write the piece, a schedule that was not uncommon.

Many nights, I would return to the paper after a meeting and file background material that I could use in the next day's story. My editors didn't expect it, but it was a way to cut corners in order to do what I had to do the next morning.

Not everyone did this. There were reporters who had real tugs-of-war with editors about the frenzied pace required to write second-day leads. Because of my situation, and because I was under so much pressure to succeed, I went to the extreme. The schedule didn't make it easy to take care of myself, and I was a wreck. I didn't eat or sleep properly. I had circles under my eyes.

But my goal was to get my stories on the front page every day. I started cracking stories left and right, and they were indeed landing on the front page.

One of the most controversial issues in town was over school financing, especially for bilingual education. The student body was primarily Hispanic, but the taxpayers were primarily Irish and there was a lot of tension in the community.

One day while reporting on a story about bilingual education for Hispanic students, a teacher made passing reference to having a bigger problem with Cambodian students. She dropped the subject, but I was intrigued and pursued it. I hadn't known that Cambodian students were even in the public schools. But I found out that a Protestant church in town had sponsored a mass adoption of about twenty Khmer-speaking Cambodian children, most of whom were orphans. A smaller group of Amerasian children from Vietnam also had been adopted.

The school system already was overwhelmed by a Hispanic population approaching 50 percent and was at a loss how to provide educational programs for twenty kids whose native language no one spoke. There simply were no teachers available to teach bilingual education in Khmer.

With the help of a couple of principals and teachers, I located the schools that the students were attending, interviewed their principals and teachers, and found out some startling facts. These kids had been tossed into regular classrooms even though they spoke no English. Their adopted families and the schools knew so little about them, including their ages, that the students had been assigned to classrooms on the basis of their stature. I discovered a sixteen-year-old girl in a sixth-grade class. I wrote a series of articles about these children, which ran on the front page for a week.

The series bred more and more articles. In the neighboring

town of South Hadley, I found four more of these kids in an elementary school, which was handling their arrival very well. The school had hired a tutor who had immigrated from Russia and who was sensitive to the notion of being in school and not knowing what was going on. I wrote a profile of her and her classroom and her relationship to the students. It was a story about how to do it right.

At the end of the six-week probationary period, the editors called me in and gave me a $50-a-week raise, which was huge at that paper.

As a result of the articles, bilingual specialists from the state education department intervened and ordered the school system to create a bilingual cluster for the students. A team of teachers was assigned to work with them and to learn about Cambodian culture. Since no one spoke the language, the school board recruited cooks and other people working in nighttime service jobs in the area to earn extra money as interpreters.

Just as meaningful as the front-page bylines, and the raise, I felt, perhaps for the first time, that action was being taken because I had bothered to ask more questions. School officials were overwhelmed. They weren't talking among themselves. But I discovered these kids, and by establishing that they were a group that had very special needs, they got assistance.

When I first started covering the education beat, I was obsessed with the politics of the school committee. I went to school committee meetings, and that was the basis on which I covered my beat. By the end of the first year, I realized that the beat was about children and education and a lot more than what seven elected people had to say about what was happening in the schools.

I also had some luck. When I graduated from the University of Massachusetts in 1984, no one in my class was getting work. It just seemed that daily newspapers wouldn't hire you right out of college—internships or no internships. Yet we all needed to get to that small newspaper where we could get a shot. At the end of my senior year I learned that *The Telegram* had openings, and I sent every clip from the newspaper where I had been working part-time, harassing *The Telegram*'s managing editor and trying to convince him that hiring a local reporter would pay off. It did.

I broke another big story because a hotshot with the state department of education had at one time been the principal of my elementary school. We had this bond, and he became a source. The school committee had all sorts of financial problems, which translated into quality-of-education problems, and this man decided that the state should intervene and take over the city's schools. Even though we were the newspaper of record, reporters at two other newspapers, a couple of television stations, and a radio station covered the town, and I had stiff competition. But he gave me the story, briefing me exclusively and helping me explain the significance of the educational takeover to readers. It was a major, controversial issue. I wrote about it for a year and a half.

It helped that I was an Irish Catholic kid from the area. Holyoke was an old mill town that was Irish in its roots. The Irish had prospered, and new people were coming to work in the mills just as the Irish once had. Now Hispanics were living in neighborhoods where the Irish had lived, and the Irish were living, literally, up the hill. Many of the Irish in the community resented *The Telegram* because they felt it had a liberal bias. They took offense at the aid and services and special education programs that the paper seemed to champion unquestionably for the new arrivals. But the minute they heard the name Cooney, heard where I was from and where I went to high school, I was in. One of the basketball coaches at the local high school was my father's first cousin; his wife taught gym; and although I never quoted them, they were good sources.

People in the community would say that other reporters were liberal do-gooders from someplace else who wouldn't listen when someone said, "I toiled in the paper mills, I pay taxes, and I feel like I have something to say about how this town is run."

When they said, "I'm losing my town; I'm losing the place that I built," I could relate to it. I didn't necessarily agree, but I could talk the talk. And that really helped me get started as a credible journalist.

Whom you sit next to can have a major effect on your job. Shortly after I arrived, the newspaper hired a woman to cover a social services beat. She was an extremely sophisticated, experienced journalist who had just gotten out of graduate school. She was smart, a good reporter, and I found myself emulating her. I would eavesdrop as she interviewed people. I listened to her talk to editors. I read her stories very carefully and would ask her to read mine before I handed them in to my editors. She took me under her wing. I started to become a better writer, not by leaps and bounds, but I spent a lot of time that year working on leads. I learned how to write faster. I learned how to write a story a day and do a good job. She was as important a person the first year as the editor who almost fired me. Sitting next to me was an example of what I wanted to be someday.

That year was a real pull-up-your socks experience. The editor I worked for, the one who wanted to fire me, said he'd never seen anyone undergo as much of a transformation as I had. I won three awards that year for my reporting, including the series on the Cambodians. Here I was, just one year out of journalism school. When he met me, he had had no faith whatsoever that I'd prove myself as a daily journalist, and he was the person who wrote letters of recommendation when I left.

I am indebted to that editor to this day, and he knows it. I hadn't been prepared to work at a daily newspaper when I walked in the door. They were giving me a reality check about the business: If you want to do this, this is what it takes. Happy hour on the Cape was not essential to my career.

Beth Cooney covers crime and law enforcement for The Advocate *in Stamford, Connecticut, where she has worked since leaving* The Transcript Telegram *in 1986. She is a summa cum laude graduate of the University of Massachusetts with a bachelor's degree in journalism and political science. She has won several awards in journalism, including first prize for spot news from the Society of Professional Journalists, Connecticut Chapter, and the Society of Silurians, New York City. She has written for* The Hampshire Gazette *and* The Amherst Record *in Massachusetts.*

2

A Ballet of Chaos

 TIMOTHY McDARRAH

This was my chance to play newspaperman. I had been working shifts as copyboy at the *New York Post*, but when a reporter who worked Sundays got sick, I was called to do a regular reporting shift.

I arrived that morning and found a large German shepherd sitting at the Sunday editor's desk in a completely dark room. His paws were flapping away at the keyboard. Lying on the floor next to him, fast asleep, snoring at three hundred decibels, was the editor, who smelled as if he'd been drinking. I gave the dog the remains of a tuna fish sandwich and took it outside to do its business. I came back upstairs with the dog, and the editor was alert and awake at the desk, scrolling through the daybook to make sure he had not snored through something on his watch. From that first moment, I knew this was the job for me.

I had grown up in a journalism environment, and it seemed like it was the only profession I ever considered. My mother had worked for *Sports Illustrated* at its beginning, has written several travel books, and is now a book reviewer for *Publishers Weekly*. My dad was the original picture editor of *The Village Voice*, and he remains there today. He would take me to the Filmore East for Doors concerts, to Miami to Democratic and Republican national political conventions, to City Hall for mayoral press conferences. Journalism seemed like an ideal way to get paid, to see things before other people did, to talk to well-known people, both famous and infamous, and then present your spin on the events to the world. Fortunately, writing came easy to me, and no other academic subject ever did.

When I arrived at the *Post* in 1985, the office was being renovated, but it was and still is a notoriously dumpy place. It is located on South Street in lower Manhattan near the FDR Drive. (In the old days newspaper offices were located near highways to avoid clogged streets and make the distribution of newspapers easier.) Smoking is prohibited, but everyone smokes anyway. There's no eating and drinking at the computer because you'll mess up the computer, but the place is knee-deep in pizza and Chinese food cartons. The decor is a gray carpet and gray Formica desks. The *Post* was built by Hearst in the 1920s and still retains that old, filthy newsroom feel.

The following Monday, I was roused from my sleep by Eric Fettman, an editor on the desk who now is the *Post*'s historian. A man named Juan Gonzalez had gone berserk with a Samurai sword on the Staten Island Ferry and had hacked a couple from Kansas, a sixteen-year-old girl, and a few other people. I drove to Staten Island, sneaked into the girl's hospital room, and got an interview, which no other paper in the city had. When I came back at the end of the day, everyone was thrilled. "Great job, Mate," the editor said. "Come back tomorrow." I was twenty-four years old and the youngest reporter. I wasn't officially on staff yet because union rules required that you work a certain number of shifts within a certain period before becoming eligible. But I was getting paid.

The *Post* then was an all-day paper, and there were deadlines every hour—eight editions, each with a different headline to trick people into buying more newspapers. I'd be called in the morning, or I would call the office from home, and editors would send me out. In the first week I covered nineteen stories. Police Officer Stephen McDonald got shot in Central Park. A Polish tall ship arrived ten days late for the Statue of Liberty celebration. The next week we got a tip that Donald Trump and Lee Iacocca were to be partners in a Florida housing development, and after writing the story, I got a nasty phone call from Trump complaining that he hadn't been treated nicely enough. He's famous for calling the media to put his spin on a story. Two days after that, I covered Daniel Ortega speaking at the U.N. and a racial attack in the Bronx. I dictated both stories from a pay phone on the street; then I went back to the office and wrote about the release of the hostage Lawrence Jenko in the Middle East.

Some people take to numbers; some are professional athletes. I excel at standing outside a police station in fourteen-degree weather, yelling, "Why did you do it?" to some rapist. That's what I do. I can also get people to say things they don't want to say. I felt totally at one with spending days on end sitting on a garbage can outside the house of Bernie Goetz, waiting for this guy who had shot at four young black men who had menaced him on a subway. In journalism, the motto is "Hurry up and wait," but if you're not ready when the moment arrives, you lose.

The *Post*, then and now, is not filled with in-depth investigative stories. There were forty or fifty reporters writing stories that ran anywhere from ten to fourteen inches. A big story was twenty-five. You learned to be very concise, to say everything you needed to say in two sentences. It was very frustrating when you had an interview with some person of note and the editors told you that a plane had crashed and to get all you could in seven inches. You'd scream at the desk, "Seven inches!" and there would be twenty other reporters on hold, yelling the same thing.

My superiors treated the whole enterprise as if it were a giant game, a very serious game, but a game. There was beer all over the office. People came and went as they pleased. I was stunned that this paper came out every day. You would never sit down with an editor and be told what you had done right or what you had done wrong. The attitude was: This is the big leagues, you're getting paid $50,000 a year (I was, with overtime), and you are expected to know what to do.

For a big story, the *Post* would gang-tackle the coverage, putting a lot of reporters on it. In January of 1987, we had the TV on and saw the space shuttle *Challenger* blow up. There was bedlam in the newsroom. The science guys were sent to Florida. Somebody else went to NASA's headquarters in Houston. Three of us went to the homes of local astronauts. The photographers did a man-on-the-street feature. It's like a ballet of chaos when something like that happens. These slovenly editors are for the most part guys who sit around and talk sports, your basic locker room crowd. But when something of that magnitude happens, it's amazing how everyone steps into line and everything gets done.

When Robert Chambers killed Jennifer Levin in Central Park, a *Post* photographer and I went to the lobby of the Mercer Street building where Jennifer had lived, and with a reporter from *Newsday* waited for her mother and father, who were divorced, to come out. And all the while I'm saying to myself, "If it were my parents, the last thing I'd want was three young punks asking how it feels that your child was just killed." But that was my job.

The mother kicked me, and the father chased me, the photographer, and the other reporter down the street, throwing packing crates at us. I laugh about it now, but if you let yourself get involved with these horrible, violent, heart-wrenching stories, you're screwed. The fact that you're such a callous, uncaring person may hurt your personal life, but it helps you as a journalist.

The first dead guy I saw was on a Sunday in August. I was sent to a theater across the street from the *The New York Times* building on Forty-third Street where a guy was standing on the fire escape screaming, waving, chanting, raving. People out on the street were screaming, "Jump, jump, splash it man, splash it!" The medical services and police arrived and started to inflate a giant air bag on the sidewalk, underneath the jumper. A priest started crawling up the fire escape, and as the second half of the air bag began to inflate, the jumper sprinted across the fire escape and made a swan dive off the fire escape, splattering on the uninflated part. His head cracked open; bloody gray matter oozed onto the sidewalk; his arm bent in such a way that his elbow was sticking out. He was less than twenty feet away from me. Everyone who was yelling "jump" went absolutely silent. Police slowly came and put a blanket over him. To this day I can still see his eyes popping out of his head.

On that day, doing this job was *not* a game. Standing inside a lobby and asking parents how they feel about their daughter dying is one thing. You don't see it. After this, when I asked about someone's dead child, or dead loved one, I'd see Raymond the jumper lying dead on the sidewalk and hear the crunch of his bones against pavement.

But a lot of upbeat assignments also came along that first year. The New York Mets got into the World Series, and I was assigned a story about ticket scalping. My editors gave me $200 to buy scalped tickets and told me to go to the game. Later that winter the Giants won the Super Bowl, and I covered their playoff games and them making a home video.

After the baseball season, we got a tip that Dwight Gooden, the Mets pitcher, had fathered an illegitimate child. I called the hospital in Florida after the editor told me that hospitals and law enforcement people outside New York City are not as suspicious as those in New York. I asked for the insurance records department and found out the child's name, the mother's name, the mother's address. I said I wanted to check the insurance records. I didn't identify myself as a reporter, but they didn't ask me. I'm hardly advocating lying, but the sin of omission can sometimes work to your advantage. I flew to Florida and got a front-page exclusive interview with the woman. We got pictures of the baby, and for the next several years I was on the Dwight Gooden beat, covering his brawl with police, his drug abuse, his stint in rehab. Dwight would see me coming, and he'd turn around and walk away.

There I was, a twenty-four-year-old destroying Dwight Gooden's personal life, and possibly his career, by finding the people who had dealt him drugs and writing about it. Now I say to myself, not only as a Met fan but as a journalist, "How could I have done this?" But then, it was a game. I'm the good guy, and you're the bad guy. If I catch you doing this, you will be publicly embarrassed before millions of people. I was given that sense from my editors. They said, "You are the eyes and the ears of the public; go get 'em. If they didn't do anything, don't get 'em." But most people have done what they're accused of.

Some reporters know how to be devious and deceptive. I was a city tabloid newspaper reporter. I just knew what one was expected to do. With four other papers in the city, sometimes one bends the rules very, very, very far. Some reporters have to be told to swipe the family pictures off the mantel of a dead person. To others, like me, it comes naturally.

In January 1987, two little boys were eaten by polar bears in

Brooklyn's Prospect Park. Someone at the paper got the address of the kids and a photographer and I went to their house. There were pictures of the boys, and not wanting the other papers to have these pictures, I took them. The *Post* had them; no one else did. I got a pat on the back. My goal was not to deprive the family of pictures of their dead relatives. My goal was to deprive the *New York Daily News*, *Newsday*, and *The New York Times* of having as good a story as we did.

I tried to maintain good relationships with the reporters from other papers, because occasionally there is sharing of information and notes. But not usually. If I wanted to get into a hospital room to talk with someone and get a picture, I might buy flowers or pizza and pose as a deliveryman. Some reporter would eventually get in there, and I felt it had to be me. If I'd show up at an address and see a particular person go into the building, I would tell the guy from the *Daily News* that he wasn't there and he'd go home. If Bernie Goetz was giving me one smidgen of information—that he was a Grateful Dead fan, for example—that tidbit, as ridiculous as it sounds, was a big story for the *Post*. So I wasn't going to share that. If Goetz was in the diner eating lunch, and the other reporter needed that detail, I'd tell him that Goetz had his grilled cheese and bacon.

Doctoring or making up quotes is something we reporters tried not to do. There's so little to gain. If you have something no one else has, and you're obviously wrong, your editor is suspicious. Sometimes we would exaggerate to have a better story. There's so much truth going on, so much that you can't make up, that to risk your professional reputation, lose your job and your personal integrity is not worth it. Yes. Tabloid reporters have integrity. Outside the industry, the *Post* is a complete joke. Within the New York media circle, the *Post* in the past has led the way with stories, because the reporters are good. The presentation may be splashy or sensational, but the *Post* doesn't make up quotes. It doesn't make up stories. It's out there. And it's all true.

I was the first one to cover the murder of Michael Griffith, who was beaten to death by a mob of whites in Howard Beach. My story in the *Post* said, "Everybody in the neighborhood knows who dunnit." Reporting is very much like police work. You go to where something happened and simply talk to everyone in sight. A TV camera light will act as a magnet or repellent. But if you're a reporter with a pen and a pad, and you buy someone a cup of coffee or a beer, it is amazing what people will say, what they will admit to if you just provide an ear. I had the whole Howard Beach case told to me by four or five kids who had heard others talking. I knew everything except the names. The police, who have the threat of subpoena and arrest, got the names.

A good guiding principle is "Be quiet." You don't have any information. They do. So let them tell you. If they're fumbling for words, repeat the last four words of what they said. The person will be prompted to keep talking.

That first year, it seemed that I was falling into some of the biggest stories. And it was customary at the *Post* to give the new guy a piece of the best ones. In March, mobster John Gotti was released from jail, and my job was to get as close as I could and report what he did during his first weekend of freedom. I followed him around, to St. John's Cemetery, where his kid is buried, to the Ravenite Social Club, where he spent time. I went to restaurants after he had been there to try to find out what he ate. I tried to talk to him, shouting questions like, "How do you feel, John? How was your dinner? How do you feel being out?" He'd look up and grunt, "I feel fine, kid, now leave me alone."

His mob guys would cut me off. One came up to me and said: "Go away—why are you here—what paper are you from—get outta here." But if they really didn't want me to follow, I wouldn't have. It was a game to me. Here I was, a twenty-four-year-old kid, within spitting distance of John and Victoria and John Gotti, Jr. It was *so* cool. The Dapper Don, the biggest mob star ever, the godfather, and my assignment was to spend a weekend with him. I was so enchanted by the whole thing.

Working at a newspaper, especially one like the *Post*, is more than a job; it's a way of life. You develop a bizarre camaraderie with the institution and with everybody you work with. You're out with them all over the place, on the street, in bars, at funeral homes. You're on call all the time. If a plane skids off a runway at four-thirty in the morning, the overnight editor thinks nothing of calling up eighteen people and telling them to go to La Guardia Airport, and Elmhurst Hospital, and the FAA office, where the grieving relatives are waiting. You just do it. You don't even say to yourself, "I'm sleeping." You get up and blindly do it. It's almost like a cult.

At the same time, it always seemed as if the *Post* was on the verge of closing. In my eight years there, from 1985 to 1993, I went through the experience five or six times. People who'd been at the paper since the late 1950s or early 1960s went through it more than fifteen times, and they were numb to the possibility. It was easy to imagine losing your job because you messed up on a story. But we always figured someone with a colossal ego and a large bank account would want to own the paper.

When Rupert Murdoch bought Channel 5, a New York TV station, U.S. Senator Ted Kennedy, who had been abused to no end by the paper, put a clause in a federal spending bill prohibiting the Federal Communications Commission from repealing a longstanding rule banning ownership of a newspaper and a TV station in the same market. Murdoch chose to sell the *Post*. The next owner, real estate developer Peter Kalikow, drove the paper to bankruptcy, and for a couple of years we found ourselves listening to our car radios or huddled around the city desk, watching the eleven o'clock news for live reports from a hotel in midtown Manhattan where negotiations between potential or current owners, Governor Mario Cuomo, and labor leaders were taking place. If they didn't strike a deal, the paper would close. But for a lot of the grizzled veterans, the attitude was "Nothin's going to happen. We'll be okay."

Eventually, the Newspaper Guild and other unions got fed up and lobbied to get Murdoch a waiver so he could get the paper back. At least his background was in publishing. Murdoch got the waiver, reacquired the *Post*, and the Guild went on strike to keep job security, seniority, vacations, and other benefits that the unions had negotiated. The other unions supported it for a few days, but they struck a deal with Murdoch, who in September 1993 fired the 287 people in the Newspaper Guild and several editors and effectively eliminated a white-collar union at the *Post*.

Everybody had assumed that if the paper closed, they would work for another paper or magazine. About a third have since returned to the *Post*, and another third have found employment elsewhere. But if you're a fifty-three-year-old art director who used to work at a newspaper, or a sixty-one-year-old federal court reporter, you won't necessarily get a job. It's very sad. When the paper went into bankruptcy, all these people lost their severance pay. People who had been there thirty or forty years and were due more than $100,000 in severance pay left with a few thousand.

I was lucky. I was young and employable. After I left, I worked on a book project with my dad about the twenty-fifth anniversary of the Stonewall riots, which marks the beginning of the gay rights movement. People at the *Post* then asked me to return, but I had the opportunity at *Dan's Papers* in the Hamptons on Long Island to run a newspaper with a circulation of over 117,000 during the season and millions in annual sales.

I had been at the *Post* for eight years. I had met everybody on earth. I could get anybody on the phone in two minutes. I had spent lifetimes camped outside murder scenes and police stations. I had done entertainment and features and gossip. I had done first-person stories, living in a homeless shelter. Director Ron Howard and actor Michael Keaton had hung around the newsroom and our local bar, talking with me, my colleagues, and my wife, who was pregnant at the time, researching their movie, *The Paper*. But there were no foreign bureaus, no investigative unit, no Sunday paper where you can write longer stories. I had done all I could do there. And now that I've left the *Post*, my wife says I'm a much sweeter person.

There's no way to put into words how it felt that first year, and every year afterward, to write for a paper read by one and a half million people, including the president. When you're in the courtroom and Claus von Bulow gets off, it sounds corny to say that you're a witness to history, but you're a witness to history. And the big reward comes when you're in the subway the next day, and you see somebody reading something that you wrote. Either you have ink in your blood, and you get a thrill from that, or you go into advertising or public relations.

Timothy McDarrah is associate publisher and editor of **Dan's Papers** *in Bridgehampton, Long Island. He worked at the* **New York Post** *for eight years. He received an undergraduate degree in urban affairs and public policy from the State University of New York at Purchase, and a master's degree in journalism from Columbia University. The book* **Gay Pride: Photographs from Stonewall to Today,** *which he edited with his father, Fred McDarrah, was published in June 1994 by Chicago Review Press.*

3

An Eye on History

 HELEN THOMAS

Washington, D.C., was where the story was. It was World War II, 1942, and I had just graduated from Wayne University, now called Wayne State, in Detroit, where I lived. The school didn't have a journalism course per se, but I majored in English, took newswriting, and worked on the college paper. I loved history and politics, and I knew that if I ever got a job as a reporter I didn't want to chase fires. Washington was where it was happening.

I went to visit my cousin in Washington and started knocking on doors. I worked in restaurants as a hostess for a year, waiting for my chance at one of the four newspapers that were thriving in Washington at the time. I was very determined to be a newspaper-woman and had a one-track mind on that. Women have been interested in journalism for 150 years, and there have always been women journalists, but they didn't get a break until World War II. Finally, there were vacancies in newspaper offices for the first time because it seemed as if the government was drafting every young man who could breathe.

After about a year, I was able to get a job as a copyboy on *The Washington Daily News* for $17.50 a week. Several months later I was made a cub reporter, and within a year, I went to the United Press, where I've been ever since.

In my first job as a copyboy, I had to fetch coffee for editors, answer telephones, cut copy off the old Teletype machines and bring it to editors. We'd watch the news come over the wires. If an important story came in, the Teletype bells would ring, and everybody jumped and ran over. I was a messenger, doing menial jobs, whatever had to be done in the newsroom. Down in the pressroom, those press people became your pals. There's no question that the people who did the scut work were the ones who were simpatico and had a sense of pride about what they were doing.

As copyboys, we hung around, soaked up the atmosphere. We kept our eyes and ears open to observe those who had already arrived. We learned who the talented writers were. Ernie Pyle, the great World War II columnist, was on the *News.* I didn't see him, except maybe once when he came home on leave. But we were all in awe of him. I was, and still am today, utterly enthralled to see great newspaper people at work. I don't think you can ever be in a newspaper office and not be amazed at how quickly some people can think on their feet. You could tell the reporters who were admired. Some could get on the telephone and get the story and then hand in copy that was wonderful to read. Or they could dictate stories on the telephone, perfect stories in perfect sentences that had a beginning, a middle, and an end. Everybody was very professional. They knew what they were doing.

When you are a reporter, you are watching history every day. And in the middle of World War II in Washington? What else could you feel? There was a great atmosphere of collegiality, a feeling that we were all in it together. There were terrible things happening. The United States was bombing the hell out of one country after another. But there wasn't anyone in our milieu who felt that the war was wrong, simply that it had to be fought and it was exacting a terrible sacrifice. President Franklin D. Roosevelt was a great leader, and there was no dissension. There was definitely a sense of unity, not only in Washington but in the whole country. I haven't had that feeling since.

All these things I was absorbing by osmosis, although I wasn't at the battle scene and I certainly wasn't editing. But just to observe what was happening, to be in that atmosphere, was thrilling. Getting your foot in the door was the main thing; it still is the main thing. If you want a job anywhere, try and be there, even if the position isn't exactly what you want. Nothing is better than firsthand experience.

The day after my twenty-first birthday, I was made a cub reporter. (The newspaper offered an apprenticeship where you could automatically move up from copyboy.) I wore my best suit to work and showed up bright- and starry-eyed. As a cub reporter, I began writing little obituaries and had the terrible task of reading the casualty rolls and calling people in the Washington area whose sons had died. Every day the government reported new casualties. The horror of it all was that sometimes we called the families before the War Department (there was no Pentagon then) had even notified them. We'd hear the screams over the phone. This was a very sobering thing. We didn't want to do it. And after a couple of times, we wanted to be sure that people had been informed. I never visited the families, but sometimes a photographer would go to the home and would pick up a photograph of the young man who had been killed. This was a war that was taking lives in incredible ways.

I'd also run out on little interviews. I certainly was not handling the major news of the day. It was local news, mainly, in Washington. *The Washington Daily News* was a tabloid. Everything was written briefly but breezily. I don't think I was nervous going out on stories. I just hoped I could do a good story. The younger reporters did have the pros around who could help us and guide us in the right direction. I learned from them how to craft a story.

Nothing can replace our experience of those days of solidarity. When a big story was breaking, everybody dropped everything else, and we all pitched in to work on it. Directing everyone was a marvelous editor who was cantankerous, but who had a respect for truth and respect for facts, the sign of a good city editor. I had had that respect before, but it was enhanced that first year. The story is the thing. It's the old cliché: You're only as good as your last story. But it's really a question of not worrying about bylines and who gets the credit. You want your paper to shine. It's that competitive spirit that we used to have. When anyone had a great story, everybody gathered around to slap the writer on the back. I was struck by how hard-boiled these pros appeared, but they always seemed to have big hearts. They were wonderful people. There was a lot of compassion under very hard shells.

There were several very tough editors. I remember they were pretty scary. They would bark at the reporters. There were several women in the newsroom at the time, but that didn't soften the editors. I don't think they were tougher on the women, but we might have thought so. We always felt that we were being judged by different standards. We were not one of the boys. At the same time, I felt that I belonged to the newspaper office, and I knew that's where I wanted to be. My editors knew that my ambition was correctly guided, but I don't think I really felt that I was taken into the inner circle.

I'm sure I made many mistakes. It was a learning game all the way, but I always blocked out my mistakes. If I didn't, I might have quit the business. I think it's always important not to become discouraged—unless the situation is fatal. I'm a cynic with hope. I always knew what I wanted to do; I had decided as a sophomore in high school when I saw my first byline in the high school paper. My ego swelled, and I said, "This has got to be it." I was never deterred from the feeling that I really loved the business.

There is a very tragic side to being a reporter, but I've never once in all my life had a thought that I had picked the wrong career. I don't think that people who go into journalism ever feel that way. They may leave for money, for higher-paying jobs. They may leave because they have to send children to college. But they always look back with longing for the salad days when they really were having a wonderful time at a job. This doesn't connect with calling people with tragic news, but with all the other wonderful things.

I never lost my enthusiasm. Sometimes I got tired. I don't think that anyone who ever went into the field in that era ever thought the workday would be eight hours. It was more like fifteen. We'd never once leave an office while a story was still going on in which we were the slightest bit involved. Even though we were members of the Newspaper Guild, we did not stick by the book and say, "It is only five days a week, eight hours a day." Anyone who goes into journalism has to know that it's about being there and having to follow through. If you want banker's hours, don't go into journalism. Stories never break on your time.

To this day, I tell my office, "Call me at any time." I have gotten calls at two or three or four in the morning. I'm glad to get them. If something is breaking that would affect my beat, particularly, I want to have that leg up and hit the deck running.

Enthusiasm, energy, alertness, dedication. If you lose your feeling of enthusiasm and think, "This isn't worth doing, what a bore," then you've lost your job. In my opinion, enthusiasm is one of the most important qualities in a good reporter. Sometimes you have to be so enthusiastic you have to sell your editors on a story. But you never lose that. You should always look at life with new eyes. I'm sure I haven't learned everything there is to know about being a good journalist. But I did learn that you should always keep your eyes open and that you can learn from any place, every day. It's a constant education. No two days are really alike. And you have to be very nosy.

I never thought the job of a reporter would be easy. But it was so exciting. And it has remained exciting. What is more exciting than news? Now, everybody has that contagion. We are a country of news junkies. The whole world is wired now. I consider news to be one of the important factors in breaking down the Berlin Wall, ending the cold war. Information. People hunger for information. One of the great things about being in journalism is that you're helping to educate people, that you really are giving them information that they need to preserve a democracy.

Unfortunately, newspapers are a dying product. I feel a tremendous sense of sadness and regret that there aren't more newspapers in every city. The world has changed immensely since I first went into newspaper work. There are different demands, but the old newspaper reporter still remains in my mind as the epitome of what journalism is all about. It took courage; it took bold steps by people who didn't care what the price was. They just wanted to be there.

So my advice is, go into the newspaper business, even if there aren't any jobs. News is being disseminated in all kinds of ways, and your skills will be needed no matter what the medium. Somewhere, somehow you will have learned a lot. Any profession that demands that you never lose hope and that really opens up the world to you is the greatest on earth.

Helen Thomas is Washington bureau chief for United Press International, where she began working in 1943 after leaving The Washington Daily News. *She has covered the White House since the administration of John F. Kennedy and was named president of the Gridiron Club, breaking the gender barrier at the once all-male club for Washington journalists. She has a degree in English from Wayne State University.*

4

Ask, and Ask Again

GOLDIE BLUMENSTYK

Even though Boston was one of the most competitive newspaper markets, I had my heart set on moving there and had even rented an apartment with a friend. But after getting my master's degree from the Columbia University Graduate School of Journalism, I landed a job as a "gofer" at the 1980 Democratic National Convention and decided to stay in New York City another month to help set up the Knight-Ridder News Service bureau. I identified the best routes between the PR offices of the Kennedy and Carter campaigns and Madison Square Garden, where the convention was held. I learned how to send copy through the fax machine, how to make sure credentials were valid, where the coffee should be located. It wasn't the sort of work for which I needed a master's degree, but just being there, around all those journalists, was great fun.

I would have gotten more out of graduate school had I gone a year or two after college. Journalism graduate school is very good for helping you understand what you don't know, for helping you think about journalism differently, and for making leaps in your career. I had selected journalism because it was public-service oriented and blended writing, creativity, and flexibility. I had worked at the college weekly at Colgate University and had worked as a stringer for the *Paterson News* in New Jersey while holding a summer job as a messenger in the paper's advertising department. But I had no career. Most of my classmates had come from schools with more sophisticated student newspapers or had already worked at newspapers, television networks, or wire services.

At the convention I met Bob Phelps, executive editor of *The Boston Globe*, to me, the most important journalist to know. I spent a week being nice to him because at the end of the week I wanted to apply for a job. On the Wednesday of the convention, I brought him my résumé and some clips. On Thursday, he said he couldn't hire me because I didn't have enough experience. However, he said I should talk to a friend of his, Jim Squires, who was expanding *The Orlando Sentinel* and hiring young reporters.

I never had any intention of living in Orlando, Florida. All I knew about Orlando was that Disney World was there. But I didn't want Bob Phelps to think I hadn't followed up on his suggestion, so I applied. Two weeks later I got a phone call inviting me to come to Orlando for a job interview.

I had spent the better part of the spring and summer going to every paper in the Boston area, being told that Northshore Weeklies newspapers would get back to me, that the *Lynn Daily Evening Item* and *The Worcester Telegram* might be interested, and that the *Quincy Patriot Ledger* might soon have a slot. But most others wouldn't even talk to me. Suddenly this paper was calling me and paying for both my plane ticket and a room at a Howard Johnson's. I went.

From the airport, the cabdriver took me on a route to the newspaper office that went along one of the seediest streets in Orlando, where topless bars and gun shops stood next to car dealerships and nearly abandoned motels. I went into the newsroom and met Jim Squires and other top editors. The newsroom was modern, just like the one in *All the President's Men*. There were desk after desk of computers. Lots of noise, raucous, even. But the staff seemed very young and excited, too. I took a writing test, feeling very intimidated and apprehensive.

Near the end of the day it became clear that they weren't considering me for a reporter's position in the main newsroom in downtown Orlando; rather, a beginner's job in a bureau in adjacent Seminole County. My heart sank. I drove out to Sanford, the county seat, with Squires's assistant. We took a highway that passed several suburbs and a lot of undeveloped land. Then we turned onto a road that ran along a big lake, Lake Monroe, where people were scattered along the banks, fishing. They looked poor, these "locals." I realized that the only place in Florida I had visited was Fort Lauderdale, which was populated with people from the Northeast and seemed more sophisticated. I didn't know anything about this rural part of central Florida.

Sanford seemed the classic small southern town. The downtown was three blocks. Near the lake were a modern city hall and county courthouse buildings. The shopping area had a few shops, a hair salon, and some variety stores, one of which had a restaurant where all the local lawyers, pols, and eventually I would go for lunches of chicken-fried steak, iced tea with free refills ("It's the South, hon'"), and pie.

Inside the bureau office was this slow-talking, pipe-smoking, Buddhalike editor named Jim Jennings. Speaking in a low, quiet voice with a bit of a Texas drawl, he told me I would be covering everything from town council meetings to chicken dinners and that I would get good experience learning about covering local government. While he talked, I kept looking around this ratty little office, with computers on folding tables and the staff photographer's pinup pictures on the walls. But what he said made sense.

So I asked him, "If you were me, and you didn't have any experience, would you think of this as a good first job?" Of course he said yes.

As Jennings spoke, I recalled a conversation I had had during the convention with another Colgate alumnus, Howard Fineman, who was writing for *Newsweek*. He had started his career working at the *Louisville Courier-Journal*. He had said to me that if you were raised on the East Coast and wanted to cover national politics, you should get out of the Northeast corridor and live somewhere that is not dominated by the New York press. You should work in a place where the newspaper is the biggest thing in the town and where what you do gets seen by people who care, and what you write about is vital to the town.

Even so, I returned to my parents' home in New Jersey thinking I didn't want the job. Two weeks later the phone rang, and I got an offer to rearrange my life and move to Orlando, where I knew not a single soul and had no friends, family, or connections. The editors told me other young reporters from out of state were being hired and I wouldn't be alone. So I took the job. But I had one final, heartbreaking task: to return to Boston and help my friend find another tenant for the apartment that I had thought would be ours.

My job was bureau reporter, writing for the "Seminole Little Sentinel," a neighborhood supplement that circulated in six residential towns in Seminole County. I was sent to the south Seminole bureau, which was then housed inside a concrete *Sentinel* printing plant, along a highway in Altamonte Springs next to an orange grove. Three other reporters worked there with me, and whenever the presses ran, we could feel the rumble at our desks.

Our only "window" was one that faced out over the plant. One day a printer threw a jelly sandwich toward the window, which stuck and remained there for weeks before anyone washed it off.

I was assigned to cover the town of Longwood, population less than 10,000, with a city hall consisting of two rooms. It had a city manager, a city clerk, a secretary, and five councilmen.

The size of a city hall definitely affects how you do your job. Much later, I became the city hall reporter in Orlando. That building had lots of offices, and you literally could spend a day going from the planning department to the public works department to the law office talking to different people, reviewing agendas for upcoming meetings, and discussing various proposals and projects. But the city hall in Longwood was basically one big room and a smaller room. There was nobody to visit. It took only ten minutes to hang out at employees' desks, and you couldn't sneak up and talk to anybody because everyone was right there in the same room.

For one of my first stories, I went to a town meeting where the council discussed getting a HUD grant and ultimately money for the town. A council member kept referring to a "hap," and I didn't realize he was talking about a "housing assistance plan." The council made no mention of housing for poor people; the councilmen thought they could get money for a senior citizens' home. I knew something was off-base, and I wrote a glib piece about how the town had no interest in housing per se; it was interested only in the money. The item was short, and I sent it via computer to Mary Ann Campbell, the section editor who was located in the main office downtown.

Mary Ann called back, asking a thousand questions: "What were the council members going to do with the money? How much money did they want? Where were they going to build this project? Who was it for? Why did they want this?" They were all very good questions, and I hadn't asked any of them.

I didn't know how to ask questions. I had never thought of myself as a shy person, but in this context I was just starting to learn that that was what you were supposed to do. Council members don't always tell you the whole story at a meeting, and they surely don't explain their motivations. It was your job to call them back, and ask why, and why, and why, and why. That was the hardest thing to learn, and it took a long time. I was still very polite. I didn't want to insult or bother anyone, and I certainly didn't want to show that I didn't know what I was talking about—the ultimate flaw in a young reporter.

Mary Ann Campbell was the classic tough-talking "newsroom broad." Each story I sent had holes in it, and she made me fill them. At the time I wasn't always convinced that her editing suggestions were the best; I used to complain that she made my stories boring. But she took out the corny stuff and made them more solid. Since then, I've learned to just ask sources: "Gosh, what are you talking about? What do you mean by that? Why is that so?" And I say it today to college presidents all day long, people who are smarter than I am, and I'm not the least bit shy about it now. I'm kind of proud to say, "I don't know what you're talking about," and make them try to explain it fifteen times, if necessary, because I think they have an obligation to explain it. But then, I had a lot to learn.

A big fight to rezone property was occurring in a neighborhood where the *Sentinel*'s editor lived. "Downtown" (the senior editors) was interested in the story, especially after we learned that a person who owned a lot of the property to be rezoned—some adjacent to the editor's house—had also helped write the new zoning law. I was especially interested in why the town had let an influential landowner and developer participate so actively in a process that affected his own property.

But I didn't understand how to gather news. I thought you had to do it on the record at a meeting. I didn't realize that you could go up to a councilman after he had voted on an issue and ask him why, and what he knew before he voted, and put the information in your story. So in the middle of a public hearing on the property rezoning, I stood up and asked the councilmen if they had known the developer owned the land when they appointed him to help rewrite the zoning law. They all knew I was a reporter, and it appeared as if I were merely crusading for my editor. Who knew? My professors didn't teach me that at Columbia.

Shortly thereafter, I got written up by a columnist in a local "shopper," which picked on my newspaper by making fun of me. Something was fishy, the columnist suggested. "Like a cork out of water, up pops Goldie Blumenstyk. . . . Most reporters wait until after the meeting to ask questions." My editors didn't get that upset, but I saw how easy it was for that (or any) reporter to make assumptions about motivation—in this case, mine—without even checking with the subject—in this case, me.

I was given a police scanner and pager, and it was exciting to hear the calls. On a Friday afternoon in January a huge fire started in Longwood. A house had been devastated. The story was to go in the metro section of the main newspaper, and a photographer from the downtown office had come to take pictures. I got to the house, and the place was a charred ruin. The owners weren't there; they had gone away for the weekend. Two nice cars were in the gutted garage, one a Jaguar, absolutely crispy.

I hung out all day, interviewing fire inspectors and the neighbors. Everyone in the neighborhood was talking about antiques in the house. I came back to the office, wrote the story, and sent it to my editor, who said it was really good. It ran on the first page of the local section. This was my first broadsheet clip, my first full-fledged story in the main paper with my name on it. It also became my first real embarrassment.

My lead said something like, "Rubble. That's what they would find when they came home that night." The *Sentinel* had a writing coach, and a month later the coach castigated one-word leads and overdramatic leads, using mine as an example. Then, six months later, the sheriff's department charged the couple with insurance fraud. They were accused of removing the valuables and setting the fire themselves. It's not that I think I should have known that when I covered the fire, and I don't think it would have changed the initial story, but I felt a little stupid. It made me a little more skeptical about what I think I know.

After nine months, I moved to the main Seminole County bureau and worked with two veteran reporters. One, Ray Lynch, taught me how to get information from court papers and property records. The other was Harry Straight, a schmoozer reporter. He taught me how he covered county government, how to develop sources, talk to them, do the chitchat and read papers upside down on someone's desk. It was fair, he said. Government employees were doing the people's business, and Florida has very strong laws requiring open public records. He taught me how to go through correspondence that came to officials each day (which was permitted by law) and to examine agendas for story leads. I would go to city hall on Thursday to prepare for a Monday meeting. I would do reporting beforehand so I'd know about the issues at the meeting. I might even write a story in advance of the meeting so people could come informed. These were the basics of government reporting.

In daily journalism, newspapers often reward people who do big projects and splashy stories. You become a star in the newsroom if you find a story and turn it into something bigger. Reporters look for that hot story, and as soon they get one, many are willing to leave everything else behind to jump on it. I believe in those big stories, too, but unfortunately the culture of the newsroom doesn't always reward people for being good, honest checks on the city they're covering. To me, that's the real test of a journalist.

Goldie Blumenstyk, who was city hall reporter for The Orlando Sentinel, *is now a senior writer at* The Chronicle of Higher Education *in Washington, D.C. She has a bachelor's degree in history from Colgate University and a master's degree from the Columbia University Graduate School of Journalism.*

5

Detail! Detail! Detail!

 MARY SCHMICH

The day before I was to leave California for England to be with the man I loved, someone at the *Peninsula Times Tribune* who had been in my graduate program at Stanford University called me and said, "You ought to apply for a job here; there are a couple of openings."

"I really have no intention of working in newspapers," I told him. I had already decided, having completed an internship at *The Los Angeles Times* and most of the course work for a master's degree in journalism, that I would spend that summer of 1980 in England with my love and then move to France, where he was from. "Why don't you just apply," my classmate said. "You never know."

I walked my application to the newspaper office and talked to the editor, Dave Burgin, who gave me a great song-and-dance routine about how fabulous newspapers were, and this one in particular.

"That's fine," I said, "but I'm leaving town now." He asked

where I was going. I didn't have the courage to tell him so I said, "Albuquerque." He asked me to leave a number where he could reach me, but I told him that wasn't convenient.

"Then call me in a month," he said.

A month later I was still in England, still considering whether to spend the rest of my life with this guy, and I called Burgin up, just to check out the possibilities. "I have a job for you," he said. "You have to come back right away."

"I can't do that," I said. "I need more time."

"You can't have more time," he said. "You have to get back here right now."

So I went back, thinking I'd go back for a little while, just to scope out the newspaper world, and here I am all these years later. I never intended to work in newspapers, ever. The idea horrified me. The only reason I went into the master's program was that a friend who thought it would be good idea sent me the application and got me financial aid.

The *Peninsula Times Tribune* was in Palo Alto. It was a little afternoon daily newspaper, which, under the editor Dave Burgin, was trying really hard to be world-class, a preposterous endeavor given its size. It was full of gung-ho people in their early to mid twenties who were out to change the world. I was in my late twenties and had been out of school for four years before I decided I wanted to try this. I felt calmer and more focused than many of the other reporters. Even though four to six years isn't much, in that first job it seemed to make a difference.

I started out covering three towns. Our circulation stretched over fourteen or fifteen communities on the peninsula of San Francisco Bay. I covered Cupertino, Los Altos, and Los Altos Hills. I went to city council meetings and to planning commission meetings. I checked with the cops every morning. I usually wrote a story every day, sometimes more. Because it was an afternoon paper, I'd often cover a meeting a night, come back to the office at eleven or midnight and write a story based on the meeting, leave the office at two in the morning, and be back in the office between six and seven so I could write for the afternoon.

It was exhausting. I was so deeply, deeply tired. About six months into it, I began to wonder when *The Los Angeles Times, The New York Times,* the *Chicago Tribune* were going to come to me and say, "We've been noticing that great work you've been doing out of the Cupertino City Council."

I hated it. I was miserable, but at the same time I was on a mission. It was amazing to me that someone who had never read newspapers could become completely consumed by working for one. I didn't want to write as often as the editors wanted me to, but now that I had found someplace that would publish my drivel, I was so excited I kept writing. It was the beginning of my fascination for places and how places work; why and how, for example, a piece of beautiful ranch land gets turned into high-density, affordable luxury condos.

This was Silicon Valley, and there were endless development issues. I'd go to the city council, and that's what the council members talked about—highways and residential developments and how they were going to get thousands of people that they were building condos for in and out of a place that had no roads.

I'd never been to a city council meeting, except for one grad school assignment. I wasn't exactly sure what a city council really did. And here I was covering city council. I remember the first one, a Cupertino City Council meeting, where they handed out an agenda. I didn't know what an agenda was; nor did I know what many of the words meant. There was this weird word that kept appearing—"ordinance." I hadn't a clue what an ordinance was. I came back to my desk after about three meetings and decided it was a word worth knowing, and I looked it up in the dictionary.

And other terms, like "impervious surface," which I realized, basically, was pavement.

At one point in my first year, I got fed up with covering meetings. I was quite full of my journalistic notions and thought the paper was far too consumed with meetings. I said to my city editor, "I'd like to try an experiment. I'd like to not cover any meetings for a month."

"What would you do?" he asked.

"I don't know, Lou, but could I try?" I said. "I'll give you a story a day. I'll just go out and find the story."

"Well, okay," he said, very skeptical. So I did, and it worked. It was hard. I didn't really have any sources, although the cops gave me a few stories. Usually, I would go out and start driving around these towns, looking for stories.

I remember the first one. I saw this weird truck parked in the little downtown of Los Altos. It was one of these makeshift trucks that the owner had nailed and taped together over the years to accommodate some purpose, and it had drawings on it. I just parked my car and got out and asked him, "What's with that truck?"

He had a traveling marionette show. It didn't make a great story, but it made a story. And it was a lot better than a Cupertino City Council meeting.

I had learned a fair amount about putting stories together in the master's program. That was the most helpful thing about the program. And I really needed it. For a class, I had gone to a city council meeting, and we were supposed to write up what happened. I wrote something like this: "At 7:01, the Palo Alto City Council began its meeting Friday. Minutes from last week's meeting were read. Councilman so-and-so announced he would have to excuse himself for half an hour." I literally wrote down every single thing.

This is where I began to have a clue that the writing I had been doing all my life in school, and that people had told me was good, was not appropriate for newspapers. I got a B- on the paper, which was generous. But I cried. I was so upset. The teacher called me in, and she said to me, "Mary, you're not writing academic papers here." She explained to me the idea of finding the most important or interesting thing and putting it at the top. This was a revelation.

The most important person that first year was Dave Burgin, the editor of the newspaper. I feel so grateful that at my first job I had a great editor. It makes all the difference in the world. And when I tell people who didn't have a great editor about what it was like in the beginning of your newspaper life to have an editor who took you in hand, it makes them all misty-eyed. And it's not just me—there's a whole rash of people who are at big newspapers around the country, who were all in kindergarten together in Palo Alto.

For example, you had to have on your desk William Strunk and E. B. White's *The Elements of Style*, Theodore Bernstein's *The Careful Writer*, a dictionary, and the AP stylebook. You just had to have those books. And you had better use them, because Dave Burgin would go through the newspaper every day and circle in red things that annoyed him, things that were wrong, or the occasional thing that he loved and then tack up those parts—all of them.

This was public humiliation. But it created an incredible sense of competition because we each knew we were the best, until something of ours appeared on that bulletin board circled in red with this big "NO!"

Dave would come by and quiz you out of Strunk and White. You'd just been to some dumb school board or city council meeting. It's one in the morning. You're sitting under fluorescent lights desperate to go home or out for a drink, and Burgin would be roaming the newsroom, looking over your shoulder to see what you were writing, picking up Strunk and White and giving you little quizzes.

He taught me and the other people who didn't resent being taught, from the beginning, how to write. I mean, really, how to write, and how to use detail. He used to shout at us from across the newsroom, "Detail! Detail! Detail!"

Toward the end of my first year I had worked my way up to general assignment reporting. My first exciting assignment was to write a profile of Joe Montana, quarterback of the San Francisco 49ers. Burgin had spotted Joe Montana as the world's greatest quarterback before he had really done anything. He was two games into the season, and Burgin said, "This guy is fabulous. Go profile him."

I set up the interview and went over to Joe's house and spent six hours there. I came back flushed with excitement. I walked into the newsroom, feeling famous because I'd interviewed a football player.

"How did it go? How'd it go?" Burgin asked me.

"I think it went pretty well," I said.

"Did you get great detail?" he asked.

"Well, yeah. Yeah, I did," I said.

"What color were his wife's eyes?" he asked.

"I—I don't know, Dave," I said in a very small voice. "I don't have a clue."

Then he started yelling at me, that if I couldn't even get something like that . . . ! To this day, I go out of my way to notice the eye color of every person I interview—and make sure I find a way to work it into the story.

For me, it was just learning by doing. I remember thinking, "I'm covering these serious meetings. I've got to write really seriously." And so I was trying to make my stories sound like the other meeting stories in the newspaper, even though I thought they were boring. (When you first start out, there's a certain element of mimicry, because you don't really know what this form is that you're dealing with.) It took me a while to understand that the other stories didn't sound all that great, and for me to mimic them wasn't serving anyone well. Having the confidence to approach stories in a different way happened gradually in that first year, and I've been dealing with it ever since.

The tug to sound like typical, boring newspaper drivel is very strong. But in the end, I started pulling myself away, thinking about what stories are and what stories are supposed to do. Where are the people in the stories? Where is the action? Where are the verbs in the story? My meeting coverage got better. I began to see that you could actually use dialogue in a meeting story. And I began to believe, which I believe to this day, that you're better served having read a lot of good fiction than you are having read mediocre journalism.

I had no intention of making this my life, but somewhere in that first year, I realized that I liked it. I really liked seeing the newspaper come off the presses every afternoon. I'd file a story at eleven in the morning, and two hours later someone would be lugging a bath of printed newspapers into the newsroom with my story in it. It was exciting.

The most exciting thing to me, the thing that made me realize I was in it for the long haul, in addition to just the thrill of seeing my writing in print, was the sense of having access to the world. All of a sudden, people whom I otherwise had no business talking to would talk to me, and whole areas of life and thought were mine to explore. Even though I had made decent grades in school, I've never been a very good scholar, and even though I'm a big reader, I've never been a very good book learner. But I could learn this way. I could learn about topics that if you had put a book about them in front of me, I'd yawn and fall asleep or turn the TV on.

The way things work. This is what newspapering teaches you. The way things work.

Mary Schmich, who is a columnist for the Chicago Tribune, *writes the syndicated Brenda Starr comic strip. She was a staff writer at* The Orlando Sentinel, *in Orlando, Florida, and at the* Peninsula Times Tribune *in Palo Alto, California. She holds a bachelor's degree in liberal arts from Pomona College in Claremont, California, and attended the master's degree program in journalism at Stanford University.*

6

The Cop Beat

 W A Y N E   D A W K I N S

My first day at *The Daily Argus*, I wrote a bylined story for the morning paper about a railroad worker who had been jolted with electricity and knocked out cold after touching the rail. I later interviewed him at his hospital bedside and wrote a follow-up story. It was quite a beginning.

I had been hired to cover the police beat, which begins at seven in the morning. The first morning at work I found it strange that reporters who didn't know me were so happy to see me. They had been taking turns filling in on the beat and were glad to see a body walk in who would handle it on a regular basis. Around noon I was in the office of Nancy Keefe, the editor, for orientation. She and the city editor, Rich Leonard, were explaining what they expected of me when one of the reporters ran in and said there had been an accident at the train station. I was told to go out there and cover the story. A more experienced reporter on the paper took me to the commuter railroad station and acted as my guide, but it was my assignment.

I started at the *The Daily Argus* in 1980 the day after Memorial Day, right after getting my master's degree from Columbia University Graduate School of Journalism. Before graduating I had received two offers, one to return to Trans-Urban News Service in Brooklyn, where I had interned after graduation from Long Island University, and one from the *Argus*, a Gannett Westchester-Rockland newspaper in Mount Vernon, located just on the edge of New York City.

I still have the pink telephone message slip from Nancy, who had telephoned me at Columbia about interviewing for a reporter's spot.

Those first few days, I learned my way around police headquarters and learned what had to be done: Go in every morning and look at the arrest book and the police reports. I also became familiar with the fire department. With my news service experience, I had done interviews in a larger venue, in New York City. But I still felt awkward. The police didn't know me. This was a smaller city, and I had to work hard during the next few months to earn their trust.

Mount Vernon, New York, is a city of about 70,000 people, one of the most densely populated cities in America. About four and a half square miles in size, it averages 15,000 people per square mile. Its density was comparable to New York City or Chicago or some of the cities in northern New Jersey, and all kinds of things happened. In other more suburban areas of New York's Westchester County, the biggest crime news was an alleged bicycle theft. Mount Vernon was cops and robbers and fires and high-speed chases. People lived close to each other, and that bred a lot of crime and ill will. There were many fires because in some parts of town the housing stock was very old and apartment buildings were built close together, making it easy for fires to spread quickly. People talk about diversity and multiculturalism, and

Mount Vernon was a classic case, going through many changes when I got there in 1980. Italian-Americans wielded political power in the school district. Irish-Americans remained a force, in the mayor's office and in the police department. But the 1980 Census reported that for the first time, the majority of residents were nonwhite and mostly black.

Mount Vernon had a police department of 170 officers, and after a while, I got to know every officer by name or to recognize their faces, from the regular beat cops and detectives to the chief of detectives to all four captains and the chief. The firefighters had a comparable force. I came in every day, five days a week, and worked every fifth or sixth weekend on Saturday. I became familiar with them. They became familiar with me.

The first major fire I covered happened just a few weeks after I began the job. A fire started in an apartment complex on the south side of town. It wasn't discovered right away, and the fire spread across three apartment houses, displacing dozens of people. By the time the firefighters got there, it seemed as if the water they were shooting into the building fed the fire rather than put it out. It burned for hours, destroying a third to a half of a city block. It was a huge story, and we played it big on the front page.

I was out there for hours. When you're young, you spend a lot of time agonizing, "What do I do first?" I just hustled to talk to as many people as possible. I interviewed people on the scene, asking how they were affected by the fire. Firefighters were coming out of the buildings, gasping for oxygen, and there I was, trying to ask questions about what it was like inside. I expected to hear, "Get the hell away from me; I don't want to talk to you." But they made an effort, once they caught their breath. I was always amazed by that, that they were willing to talk. The chief and deputy chief encouraged it. They knew you were from the local newspaper and let you get as close to the action as possible, telling you what was

going on. Being there all the time, I had an advantage over reporters working at New York City newspapers who would rush in, do
a one-shot story, and leave. At times, the police don't like what
you write. They may grill you, or freeze you out, but as their local
reporter, you're always there. You have to look these folks in the
face each day. They see you day in and day out, good or bad. That
helped get their trust.

Once I got so close to a fire the smoke soaked through my
clothes. Spray from the hoses had hit me and got on my notebook.
The ink was running off the page. When I got back to the office
to write the story, I smelled like a smoked ham, and most of the
office let me know it. The paper paid the cleaning bill. I've always
saved a copy of that story because I am partially in one of the
pictures, interviewing someone who had a role in getting someone
out of the building. I have my notebook out, and I look so serious
asking questions. Smoke is in the background. It was pretty exciting for a young reporter.

These breaking stories would drive me crazy as I wondered
every time, "Oh, my God, where do I start?" I had an adrenaline
rush and just did it. I had a job to do. If I didn't get the story, I'd
have to explain why to a very angry editor, so I dealt either with
these irritated cops or with my editor. You just try to do your job
as professionally as possible and not be obnoxious. You try not to
get in the way. If you show patience and respect, you'll get respect
back in most cases. If you are courteous, things will work out,
even in tense situations. You try to get as much as you can from
the police. But sometimes police are not cooperative. Police accounts of deaths are pretty harsh. It's the nature of how they do
things: just the facts, ma'am.

You use alternate sources, too. You talk with eyewitnesses, people in the community who may have seen what occurred. If so-
called ordinary people died, you would go to the family for more

information to put a human touch on a story—if the family was willing to cooperate. You'd get a mixed reaction, including a door slammed in your face and a "How dare you bother us!" But sometimes a family would want to talk as a catharsis. When I knock on a door, I go with a notebook in my hand, and sometimes they are more than happy to talk to me, to say, "There's more to my son or daughter." I keep thinking about a teenage girl who was killed. I interviewed her father at their house. He was soft-spoken, apparently out of shock. I was amazed that despite his grief, the father patiently answered my questions.

My first homicide story involved a young man who had been shot. When I arrived at the neighborhood, the chalk mark where the body had been was still in the street. People were describing what the gunfire sounded like. When you watch TV or a movie, guns sound like cannons or rockets. But witnesses always say they sound like firecrackers on the Fourth of July. That doesn't seem as violent, but people still die.

Covering the police and fire departments was fun, but covering crime or disasters or just bad things happening to people can wear you down. The city had seven to a dozen homicides a year. It can be depressing. The fellow before me covered the beat for about eighteen months. I was at *The Daily Argus* nearly four years and covered police about two and a half. Others burned out after a few months, they were so frustrated.

Young reporters often get assigned to cover the police beat because it requires a lot of energy. You definitely learn from it, but it's a beat that doesn't get the priority it deserves. It really deserves experienced people because it's a sensitive beat.

A lot of things in journalism you learn by osmosis. Coworkers don't tell you directly and textbooks can't teach you, but in certain situations you have to make ethical calls by trusting your instincts. No one is there to tell you the right course of action to take. In interviews, for example, you can ask official sources really tough questions because they're sophisticated about talking to the press. But it's different when talking with ordinary people, and you need to know when you may be taking advantage of them or invading their privacy. I try to make it as clear as possible that I am from the newspaper, that my intent is to write stories, and not try to mislead them. Being so eager to get a story, some reporters may misrepresent themselves.

Five or six reporters and two editors were based at this office. There was a strong New England influence at Westchester-Rockland newspapers, which felt different from my first journalism experience as an intern in Brooklyn. With hard news and fast-breaking stories, the *Argus* editors were very detail-oriented, making sure you got all the essential elements. There was so much breaking news, but if you had holes in your stories, the editors still would ask, "What about this? What about that? Was a weapon found near a crime scene?" I wouldn't be angry at the editors for asking. I'd be madder at myself for forgetting to ask in the first place. They wanted this information, so I'd pick up the phone and call or find some other way to get it. Later on, I had a better idea of what questions to ask. You have to get those important details.

One of the biggest things I learned that first year is that you have to be accurate. The *Argus* is an afternoon paper, and covering the police beat, I was the only reporter who wrote on deadline. One of the editors, Nancy Keefe, would often yell at me, even when I was writing brief items for the police notebook, about minor style rules such as when to abbreviate "street" or "avenue." It was a big thing to her. If it came down to embarrassing me in the newsroom over some error I'd made, she would do it. Aside from style, which is cosmetic, I also learned to make sure to get the facts right, the names right. Sometimes stories about events that had happened at six or seven that morning would get printed in the paper so quickly that the public could read them by eleven. When you're writing with not that much time, you have to work hard to get it right, and when you get it wrong, you hear about it—that day.

There's one mistake I always wince about. We ran a Monday feature called "Spotlight," where each reporter on a rotating basis had to write a twenty-five-inch profile of a person in the community who had done something interesting in a job or hobby. I did one on a local woman, a schoolteacher, and I spelled her name wrong throughout the story. That was terrible. This was a profile, not just a story that I had to write fast. You don't take things for granted, especially with names.

The paper also emphasized good writing. At newspapers you often have very strong writers, or very strong reporters, and some with a rare ability who are good at both gathering information and telling a story. I learned a lot about both, although I'm probably a stronger reporter. If I can go out and look at something, or interview someone face-to-face, I can craft a pretty good story. Some people can sit in their offices and turn out beautiful copy without seeing what they're writing about. I have to see it.

My editor, Nancy Keefe, would take time working with me on writing. After I was there about seven months, she left and was replaced by Steve Burgard, who also came in early and read a lot of my copy. Steve, who is now at *The Los Angeles Times*, always asked a lot of questions about facts in the story. It wasn't that he changed things. He just wanted to make sure he understood the story and that the details checked out. I knew why Steve was doing what he was doing. If something was wrong, he'd point it out and say, "Maybe you should do it this way." Some editors annoy reporters because they make changes without asking and ruin the meaning of a story. The rare times when there was time, stories would be kicked back to us, and we'd get another crack at trying to improve them. I'm grateful for that. There are a lot of reporters who think they're hotshots and who don't know how bad their copy is. I got rigorous training where I worked. When I moved on, my stories didn't have to be heavily rewritten.

I had decided to be a journalist when I was fifteen. My favorite subjects in school were social studies and English. I liked to write and read, and had developed the newspaper reading habit. I was used to seeing my parents read the paper, and I had an uncle in Panama who was a newspaperman. I started as a sportswriter in high school, covered sports in college, then switched to news stories, and eventually was an associate editor. I now have bachelor's and master's degrees in journalism, and I'm glad I do. I have some designs to teach.

At the end of my first year in Mount Vernon, I joined the National Association of Black Journalists. Recently I wrote a book, *Black Journalists, The NABJ Story*, a history of modern-day African-American journalists who have broken into mainstream journalism since the 1960s. I felt there was nothing out there that told that story.

I feel an obligation as an African-American journalist to increase our numbers in daily journalism and all parts of the craft. During my first year in Mount Vernon, I cofounded a monthly newsletter with other Columbia graduates, which still publishes, called *The Black Alumni Network*. We founded this independently. It started as a one-page typewritten sheet mailed to twenty-five of my classmates; now it's four to six pages, and we have a list of three hundred. It is paid for by subscription with no outside funding. I'm still the editor. We realized that we didn't have a lot of mentors because there hadn't been even one generation before us of African-American journalists in major media. We were tired of what we thought was a lame excuse by editors: "We can't find qualified black or Hispanic or Asian-American journalists." That's baloney. But rather than just complain, we decided to become doers and change the industry. We set up a job line so people would know of openings and qualifications. The newsletter has items about job changes and good stories that people do. We send it to anyone who wants it: Alumni, newspaper editors, people who have no connection get it. I think we've made an impact. I get calls all the time from employers who are looking to diversify their staffs. The newsletter was created because a number of people in my class shared an ideal, that we had an obligation to reach back and pull some other people up with us.

Wayne Dawkins is an assistant metro editor at the Courier-Post *in Camden/Cherry Hill, New Jersey, where he also was an editorial writer. He also writes a weekly op-ed column that covers topics such as urban issues, race relations, and diversity. He has a bachelor's degree in journalism from Long Island University and a master's degree in journalism from the Columbia University Graduate School of Journalism, where he received a distinguished alumni award in 1990. He is the author of* Black Journalists, The NABJ Story, *published by August Press.*

7

Rhythm and Dues

 A N N E G R O E R

Washington, D.C., was in the throes of the civil rights movement. It was the spring of 1967, and I had just graduated from the University of Maryland and was waiting to take a post in the public affairs division of the Smithsonian, beginning July 1. But eager to make a little money and perhaps take my last journalism job (the first was at age ten delivering a neighborhood weekly and the most recent was on my college daily), I signed on as a member of *The Washington Star* dictation bank.

Smack in the middle of a cacophonous newsroom, eight or ten of us sat in front of old, Royal manual typewriters pounding out whatever it was we heard on our headsets: obituaries from local funeral directors, afternoon stock quotes, accounts from congressional correspondents of raucous Capitol Hill floor debates or committee hearings, and, on really good days, breaking news stories from the legendary likes of Pulitzer Prize winners Mary McGrory, Miriam Ottenberg, and Haynes Johnson.

This was one of several "long hot summers" of horrendous race riots, which I greeted with awe, fear, and great sadness. Just weeks after my arrival at the *Star*, Newark was in flames, and the editors dispatched one of their most gifted writers—Haynes Johnson—to New Jersey. I will never forget the day he called in to dictate. I was absolutely thunderstruck as he unloaded paragraph after paragraph of chilling prose while the city of Newark burned.

"Where in God's name are you calling from?" I asked. "You sound so strange."

"I'm on the floor of a beauty shop in the heart of the ghetto, being hidden by the ladies who run it," he said. And I could only marvel at my great good luck in having bungled into a job that afforded not only an extraordinary ringside seat to history but a window into the mind of a great reporter. I was able to hear him think out loud, compose on the fly, and grope for the right noun or verb. Sometimes he would forget a crucial part of speech and, when reminded, was gracious enough to say, "Well, what do you think ought to go there?" I'd fill in the blank; we'd talk it over and proceed.

It was then I decided that newspapering was the way I wanted to earn my living. I had done some cutting-edge reporting at *The Diamondback* at the University of Maryland, where we ventured off campus to cover anti-Vietnam and Ku Klux Klan demonstrations and zeroed in on such backyard shockers as student drug use and the problems black students faced at an overwhelmingly white university. But I knew that nowhere else would I get the same kind of on-the-job training as I was getting from greats like Mary and Haynes in my crash course at the *Star*. Little did I suspect, however, that within one short year, this talented duo would volunteer to help me change my life.

Not every reporter was a dictation bank favorite. Some frightened us to death, like science writer Bill Hines, as graceful a word-smith as you could find but one who spoke at machine-gun speed on deadline.

Some writers made us homicidal, like Bob Lewis, who, after attending a mind-numbing zoning board or civic association meeting, would proceed to drive us mad with the slowest, most tedious monotone dictation imaginable: "At . . . the . . . top . . . of . . . the . . . page . . . please . . . put . . . 'By . . . Robert . . . J. . . . Lewis . . . *Star* . . . staff . . . writer.' " That intro alone seemed to take five minutes. You could always tell who had Bob on the phone by the rolling eyeballs and near somnolence of the dictationist.

But he couldn't hold a candle to one correspondent who usually called around eight in the evening and nearly always sounded as if he had a perfectly chilled martini in one hand and a voluptuous female in the other. He never actually said as much, but we took it on faith that that was the drill. There we were, young geeks in a newsroom, eating soggy, cardboard food and drinking nasty coffee, and this guy was lounging around like some journalistic Hugh Hefner.

We made our own entertainment. We frequently invited one of the city editors, Boris Weintraub, to the dictation bank during afternoon doldrums (after the morning deadline crunch) to read us the doggerel du jour. Most days it was mediocre rhyme by Vincent Godfrey Burns, poet laureate of Maryland, and always it was delivered in a style worthy of Oscar Wilde.

On particularly slow days, we'd crank up the Dictation Bank Rhythm Band under the able direction of one Cotton Kent, a rock-and-roll guitarist who for a few brief years sought to follow the footsteps of his father, Carlton Kent, a veteran newsman, until he decided instead, and quite rightly I think, to follow his own muse. Cotton had a great ear, a liquid baritone, and a mighty sense of the absurd. As he waved his conductor's baton (a copy pencil), we would beat pica sticks on the desk, shift typewriter carriages to ring the bells, and otherwise launch into high percussion until ordered to stop by a humorless editor.

Even amid the hijinks, we managed to fathom a great deal: how to think on deadline. We listened over and over to seasoned reporters as they grappled with breaking news stories or, after running the length of the cavernous newsroom, pitched story ideas to editors. You could learn much about crime reporting simply by cocking an ear in the direction of Charlie McAleer. Late each evening, he called every local police force (there were nearly a dozen in the Washington area) to inquire, "Who's dead? Got any action tonight?"

After six delicious weeks at the *Star*, I was reluctantly preparing to say farewell and take my job as a junior member of the Smithsonian's public affairs staff. Although I had sworn I would never do public relations, the Smithsonian was no ordinary spin shop, as I had learned during a summer internship the previous year. But when the man who was to have been my boss called to say, "I have really bad news. Congress didn't appropriate money for your position and so we can't pay you," I had only one reply.

"This is wonderful," I said. "I was a little concerned about how to tell you I'd rather do night cops than write press releases about eighteenth-century Venetian artists." That Smithsonian un-boss became an Interior Department official and for more than twenty-five years was one of my best bureaucratic sources.

The *Star* had a system that allowed dictationists to become re-porters through a training program; you were tapped if you showed genuine motivation and talent. One way to prove your enterprise, after a day shift taking dictation, was to volunteer for a night assignment considered too minor for a "real" reporter but important enough to warrant some kind of coverage. As an incen-tive, they paid $15 per assignment, which was heavy-duty entice-ment considering I was earning the princely sum of $65 a week.

My first assignment was a speech entitled "The Medium Is the Message," by new-age communications guru Marshall McLuhan. I was thrilled and for nearly an hour wrote down virtually every word he uttered. I did so in shorthand, which I had learned in high school. It took me nearly four hours to transcribe what he had said and another three hours to figure out what to write. I filed a six-hundred-word story that was cut by two-thirds, adding devastation to exhaustion. But I learned several invaluable lessons: Always ask event organizers if there is a prepared text, from which you can select two or three key quotes in about ten minutes; use a tape recorder with a good fast-forward function; and try to do a little pre-event research so you have at least a glimmer of meaning in all that talk.

The McLuhan speech was an exception to the usual nightly fare of civic associations, business groups, and, increasingly, civil rights rallies and strategy sessions for the upcoming Poor Peoples' Campaign and Resurrection City—a massive march on Washington to protest racial injustice and poverty—culminating in the construction and occupation of hundreds of temporary shelters on the Mall.

Editors had no qualms about sending me to ghetto churches and storefront headquarters, and I was ever so eager to go. I knew that if I did this long enough, I would have to be selected as a trainee and then could be assigned to the safer venues of city hall and superior court during daylight hours. But after seven or eight months, I realized that each new trainee was always a man, never a woman.

The city editor was a crusty old marine named Sid Epstein, and I finally went to his office and told him face-to-face, "I want to be a city-side reporter."

"I don't want any girls on my city desk," he shot back.

I was stunned. "But this is my city," I insisted. "I was born here. I grew up in Washington. I live here, and this is what I want to do."

"Well, you can work in the women's section or in the suburbs. But the city is just too dangerous," he said. "There is all this civil rights stuff going on, and you could get hurt."

I really wanted to say, "I wouldn't be caught dead back in 'society,' " which was the precursor to today's gender-neutral "lifestyle" sections. But I couldn't trash his suggestion since the fashion editor was his wife.

To be sure, there were several women reporters working for Sid: Shirley Elder, who covered Congress; Miriam Ottenberg, who won a Pulitzer for uncovering widespread used-car fraud; and Myra McPherson, a gifted news and feature writer. But basically, women were not to be city-side reporters. Martha Angle, now at *Congressional Quarterly*, spent a goodly number of her *Star* years in the suburbs before graduating to Capitol Hill. But too many talented women were writing behind a pink curtain in "society." The closest they could get to hard news was embassy parties and the First Lady. Brenda Starr never had these problems, and I was growing increasingly depressed.

Leaving a job you love, even if there are aspects of it you hate, is never easy. But the handwriting was clearly on the wall. At one point I was assigned to cover the opening of a psychedelic music hall in Adams-Morgan, a neighborhood that was then a little dicey, although the closest place Washington would ever have to a hip melting pot. The Ambassador Theater was Washington's answer to San Francisco's Avalon Ballroom, where rock musicians often took a backseat to light shows and other techno-theatrics designed for a generation of flower-power hippies. About two hours before concert time, Sid sent word through an editor that I was being pulled off a story that I loved, so they could send rock-and-roll writer Mike Oberman, who, for the record, had no desire to be there. The reason for the switch: Sid feared it might be unsafe. Since I lived just five blocks from the theater, I found this absurd. I ran a far greater risk of being mugged walking after dark from the *Star* building to my car.

So Mike and I made a deal: We'd pretend we never got the messages. I went to the opening, wrote the piece, and it ran in the Saturday paper. I felt pretty smug. I was on the dictation bank Saturday morning when Sid came in. He had seen the paper and was livid. He went into his office, and I could see him through the glass partition. As he sat down, he winced in pain, and I knew he was having another bout of chronic back trouble. This was a bad sign. He was already irritable. He summoned me into his office and, rising to his full six feet, growled at me as if he were back on Parris Island: "I should fire you for this! How dare you defy me!"

Terrified, I could only squeak, "Sid, someday you're going to think this was awfully enterprising on my part." But I knew that day would never come. I had crossed him royally, and I had rejected out of hand any offer to cover suburban school board meetings or parties on Embassy Row. My only option was to leave—honorably. I had no idea where to go. There were two other newspapers in Washington in 1968—*The Washington Post* and *The Washington Daily News*. But I didn't think I had enough experience to apply for a reporting job, and I vowed my clerking days were over.

However, help was closer at hand than I imagined. There, on the *Star* bulletin board, was a notice from the University of Wisconsin touting its Russell Sage Fellowship, specifically designed for recent journalism school graduates who, like me, had majored in journalism instead of something useful like economics, Soviet history, or agriculture policy. There were eight or ten openings, a generous stipend, and the chance to spend a year in the Midwest at one of the best, and most interesting, universities in the country.

This was the "respectable" exit of my dreams. Although my personal drama was playing itself out at the height of the civil rights movement—when race discrimination suits were coming to the fore—it never occurred to me that there also could be such a thing as a sex discrimination action. And since my name wasn't Barry or Winston or Steve, I decided to go back to school. I turned for advice to Haynes Johnson, who, as luck would have it, did his undergrad work at Wisconsin, and to Mary McGrory. They were enthusiastic and supportive.

"When you finish writing your application, Mary and I would be happy to look it over and offer a little gratuitous advice," said Haynes, with whom I had developed a wonderfully close mentor-protégé relationship that endures to this day. So I gathered up my papers and walked to the back of the room, and for the next half hour, these two Pulitzer Prize winners carefully read my grad school application while I silently thought, "This is probably the highest-priced editing I'll ever get."

I was accepted in April of 1968, largely, I believe, on the strength of my application and my references—Haynes and Mary. I left the *Star* in August to embark on another phase of my journalistic life. But in some ways, my year at the *Star* was the most extraordinary.

This was a newsroom that was part *Front Page* and part "Lou Grant." Most of the people there considered journalism a calling, not a job or a trade. These were men and women who worked their sources assiduously, and it paid off. Jerry O'Leary, for example, was the first reporter in the country to be told the identity of Martin Luther King, Jr.'s, assassin—from a pal at the FBI.

I also learned a great deal about the human condition because a newsroom, like a foxhole, breeds great camaraderie. We helped one newsroom chum study her catechism before her prewedding conversion to Catholicism and tried to make another of our pals understand he had a serious drinking problem.

The *Star* died in 1981, thirteen years after I had left, and its alumni are scattered around the world. Some are still writing for newspapers or magazines. Others are in television, radio, or public relations. Cotton Kent, at last report, was making music in Los Angeles. Robert J. Lewis, *Star* staff writer, has gone to that great composing room in the sky. One fellow dictationist, after a distinguished career at *Time* magazine, opened a successful chain of Italian restaurants in Hong Kong. Sid Epstein, now retired, does occasional newspaper consulting work. Whatever and wherever we are, we share an abiding love for the *Star*.

It was there in that grungy newsroom that I was transformed from an eager, industrious, just-out-of-college cub into a tough, tenacious reporter. After all, if I could stand up to Sid and live to tell about it, a president of the United States would be a pushover.

Anne Groer is a national correspondent in The Orlando Sentinel *Washington bureau, which she joined in 1974. She worked for the* Washington Daily News *from 1970 until it folded in 1972. She traveled extensively in Europe and Latin America before joining the* Sentinel. *A veteran political correspondent, she was a panelist in the first George Bush– Michael Dukakis nationally televised presidential debate. She holds a bachelor's degree in journalism from the University of Maryland and was a Russell Sage Graduate Fellow at the University of Wisconsin.*

8

Clarity Above All

 CRAIG NEFF

There's a certain panic that sets in when you're fresh out of college and have to get two or three stories done in six hours. You figure out ways as if your life depended on it, thinking you'll lose your job if you can't track down a particular person. You get carried through on adrenaline.

I came out of Colgate University in May of 1979 and applied to small newspapers, figuring that the first place that offered me a job was where I would start. An afternoon daily newspaper in Torrington, Connecticut, *The Register*, hired me as a general assignment reporter. It was a small staff in a place where everyone worked day and night. I covered zoning board meetings, school board meetings, and sewer commission meetings until eleven-thirty at night and then returned to the office by six the next morning, working on two or three stories for my noon deadline.

About a month after I started in Torrington I got a call from the chief of reporters at *Sports Illustrated* that the magazine had an opening in its research department, where I had spent the summer after my junior year working as an intern-reporter-researcher. I was getting paid $7,200 a year by the newspaper, and I was happy to move on.

I'm one of those people influenced to go into journalism by Bob Woodward and Carl Bernstein. While in high school I started an underground school newspaper with a friend whose father was a newspaper publisher. In college, because I'd always played sports and knew a lot about them, and because there was a vacancy, I became sports editor—and eventually executive editor—of my college weekly.

My newspaper experience in Torrington did not even touch on sports, but it was great training trying to juggle multiple stories at once, to focus on important questions, and to track down sources that I needed to reach by phone in a hurry, sometimes waking people up early in the morning. I was glad I had only a month on that job, because I would have died from lack of sleep.

At *Sports Illustrated* I worked as what the magazine staff called a reporter. My number-one job was to fact-check stories by staff writers. We would work Thursday through Monday because of weekend sports events. I'd get a feature story on Thursday morning and have to get that done by Saturday. I would get a news story on Sunday morning and be done by Sunday evening. I had to recheck every fact and thoroughly discredit it or prove it by looking at various books and magazines, or by telephone interviews, often by calling the direct, original source of the information. I had to make sure that every single word in the article was completely accurate—both factually and in its implications. The story had to have a proper tone and couldn't be misleading or legally unsound.

The chief of reporters taught me which sources were considered most credible. There was a system of black checks and red checks. A red-check source was considered essentially infallible, or close to infallible. Those would be original sources. If we were quoting someone's opinion in the magazine and a fact checker asked that person his opinion, you could trust him to know his own opinion. Certain resource books and past issues of Time Inc. publications also were considered red checks because the articles had gone through the rigorous fact-checking process. A daily newspaper or an encyclopedia would be considered a black check. You needed two independent black checks to equal a red check, so you usually needed two sources for everything.

During that year I developed a heightened respect for accuracy and how difficult it is to write a completely accurate story. In the process of checking stories, I would read newspapers or books that were just riddled with mistakes. It was depressing to see how many errors there are even in very respectable daily newspapers, even the biggest-name newspapers.

Since then, I've tried to use that same fact-checker precision in pinning down interview subjects. When they make a blanket statement, I try to make sure that each part is correct and not some bit of wisdom that's been passed along or that somebody heard thirdhand. In journalism, a lot of inaccurate information gets reprinted and goes into the food chain and becomes reality. I've learned not to assume that things I've heard often are necessarily true.

Fact checking more or less destroyed my ability to read faster than two words per minute. I'd read a newspaper, I'd read a novel, and be asking myself, "Now I'm not sure that's factually correct. I wonder what the source for this is." I became skeptical of every word I read.

I was based in New York in *Sports Illustrated*'s offices, doing my checking. Writers were, most of the time, at an event somewhere else in the country. Reporters tended to fact-check by beats. One of my first was track-and-field and Olympic sports. I would work with the same writers fairly often, and we developed a good rapport. Sundays, the closing day of the magazine, were the real pressure cooker, especially if the piece I was checking was controversial or investigative. I'd get my story in the morning and start calling and researching as much as I could. By the end of the day, I had to have all the checking done. It wasn't always easy to track people down on Sundays. No one's in his or her office. I had to rely on the writer of the story to collect phone numbers for me, or I had to anticipate what might be in the story. I'd often call someone the Friday before and say, "Is there some place we might be able to reach you this weekend? I think we might be writing a story that relates to you."

Writers had to file Saturday sports events first thing Sunday morning. They would stay up all night writing and would want to sleep all day, and didn't always like it when I had questions. The writers were uneven. Some were great to work with and extremely accurate. Some I had to check extra hard because they'd take a little more license with the material. Reputations got around the office, so people would warn me, "This guy plays a little fast and loose with the facts." Sometimes when I challenged a writer, he or she would say, "Well, somebody told me that; I can't really remember who it was." It would turn out it was an unprovable fact, and probably was an untrue statement, and I would just take it out of the story. In the end, we, the reporters, were responsible for every word that went into the magazine. The writer wasn't blamed; the reporter was. So we knew that we couldn't make any blunders.

When I was two-thirds through the checking process, I would hand over my checking information to the senior editor on the story, who would move the story through a couple of top editors at the magazine. There were times when at two or three in the morning, an editor would suddenly realize that he needed another piece of information. The person who could give me that piece was usually someone I had to call on the phone, and that was the worst part, having to wake people up in the middle of the night for some question like, "Which finger were you wearing your championship ring on?" It was sometimes extremely silly stuff. In some cases I was lucky, and the person was on good terms with the magazine and had dealt with the staff before, and had gotten awakened at two in the morning before. Sometimes people would be very grumpy, and occasionally would say, "Call me tomorrow," and hang up. I'd have to fight it out with the editor whether this piece of information really had to be in the story since there was no point in calling back. Every once in a while I'd have to do a little bit of fudging; rather than put in something wrong, I'd take it out or find some way to write around it.

On Sunday nights, at least two-thirds of the staff of twenty reporters were there. The magazine was still humming, a little groggily, but still alive. We built a certain camaraderie staying late. It was a little like being there all night at the weekly paper in college. We'd order in Chinese food and end up watching bad movies in someone's office. By two o'clock, a story had basically been checked, but we couldn't go home until it had been read by the right person for the final time. We'd end up at the office until three or four in the morning before the magazine would be closed.

It was a weird lifestyle because of the workweek. We worked Thursday through Monday, and Tuesday and Wednesday were the weekend days. It was difficult to have a normal social life because no one else is off Tuesday and Wednesday. They were great days for doing laundry and seeing movies without having to wait in line. We ended up socializing a lot with our work colleagues. It was good up to a point; it formed a certain bond that has carried on, and I have many, many friendships from that first year, but it's not a very normal life, if journalism ever is.

Checking was one part of the job. Another was actually going out to events or making calls from the office to help a writer in the original research. The first event I went to was the World Cup track-and-field event in Montreal. I was working with Kenny Moore, who was an Olympic marathoner and had been *SI*'s head track-and-field writer for a long time. He would send me off to interview the winner of a certain race because track meets tend to be very hectic; the races occur one after the other. No one person can reach all the coaches, winners, and losers. I got sent into the stands to chase down the head of the International Track and Field Federation—a crotchety, old, very unpopular figure who didn't like reporters. I was able to get a couple of quotes out of him and thought that was a real triumph. It was in the Olympic Stadium in Montreal, and I was in heaven. I had remembered watching the 1976 Olympics, which had taken place there. I was so determined to do a good job. I think I did.

I also traveled to Philadelphia to cover a track meet and to Los Angeles for another story. I would have a portable typewriter along with me—this was before the days of computers—and either type out my notes or sit with my notebook and the writer, who would ask, "Did you talk with so-and-so?" I'd read key quotes, which the writer might copy into a notebook. Each writer had an individual style when dealing with reporters.

I was assigned to the 1980 Summer Olympics in Moscow, but the U.S. boycott ended that trip. Instead, I traveled in the Northeast to interview athletes and get feedback on the boycott. I talked by phone to people in the Carter White House, to pin them down on their plans and thinking behind the boycott. I did get to write a two-page preview of the events that were scheduled in Moscow. Now *Sports Illustrated* does 250-page Olympic previews.

I was scared to death in some of my first interviews. I had to tune out my nerves and ask my questions and not seem ignorant or green or in any way cowed by the experience. Even for a veteran reporter, it can be a pain in the neck to talk to athletes. Reporters are generally unwelcome in the locker room, which athletes consider to be their private territory. Reporters must be as professional as possible, not get into arguments if the athletes won't answer certain questions, remain polite and straightforward, and ask bright questions. But there's no such thing as an inherently stupid question if it elicits an interesting response or even a heated response because the player thinks it's dumb. One writer I worked with during my first year liked to boil down and simplify points. He'd ask almost uneducated questions, even if he knew the answer, because he wanted the basic elements of the story explained for the reader by the coach or athlete.

When interviewing a marathon runner, rather than coming up with some convoluted, drawn-out question that confuses the subject: "Did you go into oxygen debt at the twenty-third mile?" the writer might ask a marathon runner, "Does it hurt to run a marathon?" You can assume so, having watched marathons and seen athletes grimace and in great pain. But the runner then says, "Oh, man, it's the most painful thing you can do," and you've got a great element in your story, described by the runner. Interview subjects in general like a nice simple, straightforward question.

I learned about writing just from working closely with writers and their copy and seeing how they put all the facts together, how they selected details that were significant, which is such a key part of journalism. In checking a story, I would actually get to know the subject as well as the writer did, and often better, and I could imagine the story I'd have written, based on the material.

If it's a news story, you've got to find the story line, and at a lot of sports events, there is more than one winner. At a basketball game or football game, only one team wins, but a track-and-field event may have a dozen events, each with its own winner. You have to figure out which performances were the most significant or what was the most memorable occurrence. Even within a football game or basketball game, you have to explain the way in which the team won. Was this guy the star, was that guy the star? Was there some outside factor that played in the team's favor for that one game? Was there something outstanding about the setting in which the game was played that made it unusual? You always come back from an event with your notebook overflowing with facts. Somehow you have to be able to focus in on the most significant handful of facts to form the core of your story.

SI's method of doing feature stories is to have a writer spend a week with a subject. During that time, you learn much more than you possibly can put into a story. A lot of it is insignificant. You have to look for the details that are very telling, that show a deeper trait of your subject—personal habits, the fact that an athlete has habits, or doesn't have habits, or is quick to anger. It's a matter of culling those crucial nuggets that will help the reader form the correct picture instead of just dumping a lot of facts into the story.

Identifying the telling detail is something you can learn if you work with a writer or editor who's good at it. I was lucky to have worked with some my first year. It can also be instinctual. There are some people who have the eye for it because they've read a lot and have a good sense of what makes a good story, or they're a good judge of character and can automatically pull out those traits. But I definitely think, having worked with a lot of people here and helping develop other people's careers, that you can, over the course of a year or few years, start to develop that crucial journalistic eye of what's news and what isn't, what's significant and what isn't. It's easier if you're born with it, but not everyone is.

When I was checking a story, I always tried to poke around a little bit, to flesh out the picture. The fact that I was checking the story a day or two after the writer had written it gave the subject a little time to step back from his or her achievements and have a deeper perspective on them. Occasionally I would make a suggestion to the editor that the writer had overlooked—a detail that I thought was interesting—and it would get put into a story. If I ended up getting a really good quote, I would always show it to the editor. Sometimes it wouldn't fit. But I wanted to help the editor get as full an understanding of a story as I had gotten.

The art of paring down was something I learned from observing how editors worked, eliminating clutter and unnecessary words. In almost every story the editor would have to cut a reasonable amount. In many cases, stories can be improved by being shortened. There's more there than you want to communicate. You'll get a clearer picture of the individual by showing a little bit less—showing those five key details and not everything that's in your notebook. I also watched the more skilled editors show their talent for finding the right word that a writer hadn't come up with.

At *Sports Illustrated*, the emphasis on clarity was constant and very powerful. There would always be one editor, of the several who read a story, who would just say, "I don't get this. We have to clarify this." It was always a matter of being a little more precise, a little more focused, and that has stuck with me. Later on, when I became a writer at *Sports Illustrated*, I knew my copy would go through this mill. I wanted to make it clear myself rather than have someone else do it in his or her words. I guess clarity above all. That's the lesson I learned.

That first year certainly helped me, because I understand the process that all stories go through. I lived it at *SI* as a reporter, writer, and editor. Now, as editor of *Sports Illustrated for Kids*, I'm the one demanding clarity and accuracy. Because of my experience,

I'm sympathetic when asking a reporter to answer my picky, pain-in-the-neck questions, but I have to be merciless. If I want something in the story that's not there, it's up to the reporter to track it down. That's the way life is in journalism; the reporter has to find the answers.

Craig Neff is managing editor of Sports Illustrated for Kids, *a monthly magazine that focuses on sports while promoting literacy. Shortly after graduating from Colgate University in 1979 with a degree in political science, he joined the staff of* Sports Illustrated, *where he worked for eleven years as a reporter, writer, and senior editor, covering many subjects, primarily Olympic sports and major league baseball.*

9

You'll Eventually Get a Break

 G R A H A M   H O V E Y

President Roosevelt was on a swing to the Northwest in the fall of 1937, ostensibly to dedicate New Deal public works projects but more likely to mend political fences damaged by the defeat in the Senate of his so-called court-packing bill that summer. I went to the railroad station in St. Paul and used my *Minnesota Daily* press card to clear police and Secret Service inspection and get close to the Roosevelt train. This was the beginning of my senior year at the University of Minnesota, and it was a tremendous thrill. I had worked through the crowd and was standing twenty feet from the rear of the train. Never having seen Roosevelt close up, I was shocked at how crippled he was as I watched him struggle across a makeshift bridge to the speaking platform, tightly grasping the arms of his son, James, and another aide. But I could observe that strong, confident face and hear the magnificent voice that had transformed political oratory in America, and witness the sheer joy he took from rousing his partisans on the campaign trail. Although I didn't recognize anyone, I was probably taking notes and rubbing elbows with some of the biggest names in journalism.

I had drifted aimlessly from one field to another, then stumbled into college journalism almost by accident while attending Iowa State Teachers College (now the University of Northern Iowa). I was on the varsity track team when a vacancy occurred for sports editor of the college weekly. I applied and, somewhat to my surprise, got the job that set me, more or less, on course. Later, as managing editor, I went to the national convention of the Associated Collegiate Press in Chicago, where in the fall of 1935 I heard two respected foreign correspondents say that a general war was coming in Europe. Leland Stowe, a Pulitzer Prize–winning correspondent at the *New York Herald Tribune*, advised all of us who crowded around him, picking up any crumb of advice on how to get such a job, that "if you want it badly enough, you'll eventually get a break." He also told us, "Don't overlook the wire services." Five years later I would meet Leland Stowe again in Africa, remind him of the student convention and that I had taken his advice, and was now on my way to cover the war in North Africa for International News Service, one of the three major U.S. wire services, a rival of the Associated Press and United Press. The inspiration of the Chicago convention had pointed me in the direction of world affairs. It also led me to transfer to the University of Minnesota journalism program where I had the opportunity to work for the *Minnesota Daily*, which advertised itself in those days as "the world's largest college newspaper."

With only one course to complete for my bachelor's degree, I left Minnesota in April 1938 to return to my home in Iowa and work as a reporter on the *Waterloo Daily Courier*, then a newspaper of 33,000 circulation in a community of 55,000 (and now called *The Waterloo-Cedar Falls Courier*). A recession was gathering momentum, and newspaper jobs were especially hard to come by. When the *Courier* beckoned, my simpatico professor said I could finish the course by correspondence. I was desperately eager to get started on a career, realized I was lucky to have that crucial first job, and knew I could learn from my *Courier* colleagues. On a bright spring day I dropped by the *Minnesota Daily* offices, then took a long walk down the green mall and across the Mississippi on the Washington Avenue bridge to catch a streetcar that would take me out to U.S. 65 to hitchhike the two hundred miles back home.

All the *Courier* had guaranteed was five months of work during one editor's medical leave and the summer vacation season, but the managing editor said he hoped for developments that would enable him to keep me on a regular basis, and this was good enough for me. The pay was $25 a week, and the position was one of the best-paying news jobs any Minnesota journalism graduate would get in that recession year. I had worked as a *Courier* reporter during summer vacations in 1937 and was glad to be welcomed back.

The city editor, Burton Burritt, was a kind of genius who had completed his course work for a Ph.D. in English at Northwestern University, then defected to journalism. He was bitterly frustrated all his life by the worst stammer I had ever encountered, and reporters were sometimes handy targets for the venting of that frustration. Burton always presided at the city desk clenching an unlighted cigar between his teeth, an implausible *Front Page* prop for a genuinely erudite editor, and I always wondered if the rarely lit Havana filled some psychological need for the stutterer. Our relationship would always be an unpredictable, up-and-down proposition, but he did pick up where my Minnesota professor, Mitchell V. Charnley, a genius for hooking students on words, had left off. Charnley had tried to teach us, in the words of the great sportswriter Red Smith, that "the English language, if handled with respect, rarely if ever poisons the user."

Burton also dazzled me on occasion with a photographic memory of events that, for a fledgling reporter, could turn an ordinary story into a good one, adding legitimate spice to it. On a Saturday night while working the late shift, covering general assignments for the Sunday newspaper, I picked up a brief notice from a funeral home of the death of a very old black woman in Waterloo. But my routine obituary struck a chord with Burritt. "I believe she was born into a slave family in the South during the Civil War," he said. "I think we carried a story about her two years ago in February—I believe it was February 18." He was exactly right. I found the story under that date in the newspaper file and borrowed liberally from it. Burritt's memory had enhanced my admiration for him and given me a good Sunday feature.

Having bought out its livelier competitor in the depth of the Depression in 1931, the *Courier* was a rich, complacent newspaper not given to aggressive coverage, reluctant ever to tangle with the city's power barons or to offend an advertiser. It would ignore as long as possible any scandal involving the older, richer families. The *Courier's* only competition came episodically from *The Des Moines Register*. Almost from day one on the *Courier* I regarded the *Register* as my logical next step, and I would drive the hundred miles every so often to make my case to the *Register's* managing editor and leave my clips. But what I really wanted, above any other job in the world, was to be a foreign correspondent for the *Chicago Daily News*.

For the present, however, my job was reporting in Waterloo. And I was to learn most about that from Frank B. Allen, a wonderful human being but something of a misfit because his heart belonged to the sprightlier *Waterloo Tribune*, where he had put in happy years before it sold out to the *Courier*. Give Frank a few hours, and he could dig out almost anything going on in and around Waterloo. When the *Courier* ran into trouble trying to get information, it would call on him. He could substitute ably on any of the reporting beats, especially at the courthouse or city hall, but the *Courier* rarely made use of his talent.

Once I was assigned a story about the Rath packing company, which was expanding its capacity. We were just pulling out of the Depression, and this was big news. I went to the plant and upon my return realized I was missing an important detail, the amount of the contract bid. I called the president, who refused to give even a ballpark figure. Frank Allen, who was hanging around the city desk, overheard the conversation and because he knew people at the companies that had bid, obtained the number from an unsuccessful bidder.

On several occasions, I watched him work the phones, starting from scratch, but knowing people who would be in on a decision, then badgering, cajoling, and implying that we knew more than we did in order to get information. He then went back to the original source, who confirmed what he had found out. He could always find someone who would talk.

But if Allen was the best reporter—the premier news gatherer—on the *Courier*, the best writer, in my judgment, was Merrill Swedlund, about eight years my senior, who shared the city editor's penchant for precise, effective English. By both example and editing, when he filled in on the city desk, Merrill helped to improve mine. He cared about writing, precision, and good word choice. So did Marjorie, the proofreader who was to become his wife, a stickler for basic grammar, a critic of hyperbole. With his interest in the arts, Merrill would have made a fine critical writer.

Eventually, I got a crack at most of the jobs in the newsroom, but I began on the East Commercial beat—all of Waterloo on the east side of the Cedar River, which bisected the downtown business area, except for the city hall and the Black Hawk County courthouse. I filled in on the sports desk, where I had done my first work for the *Courier* as a stringer in Cedar Falls.

The telegraph desk was run by Ed Wood, a colorful old-timer who had worked in many parts of the country before coming to roost in Waterloo. Woody was the only *Courier* editor to wear the traditional green eyeshade. He worked hard at his curmudgeonly mien, and he could savage his younger colleagues with picturesque language just as they were trying to get a headline to fit on deadline. Beneath the crust was a kind man with sympathy for beginners. Woody feuded zestfully with Burton, often needling him. One day the needling hit a nerve, and Burton came roaring out from behind the city desk to provide a sight for a shocked newsroom, stuttering incoherently, arms flailing, unlit cigar flying off into space, while Woody, obviously relishing his coup, gazed calmly at the quivering Burton as though he could not imagine what had provoked the city editor's wrath. Burton finally realized what a spectacle he was making and stalked glumly back to his desk, his face, naturally red at normal temperature, now a crimson flush.

The *Courier's* editorial page was bland beyond belief, and I did not envy our one editorial writer, but when he left I applied for the job with no expectation of getting it. I was asked to fill in during the interim and saw that the job in that stultifying intellectual climate would be endlessly frustrating. I only enjoyed writing the short, offbeat edits that filled out the column and trying now and again to sneak in an editorial on politics containing a few camouflaged overtones. When I did go into editorial writing fulltime many years later, I was fortunate indeed to have great editors, Wilbur Elston at the *Minneapolis Star-Tribune* and John B. Oakes at *The New York Times.*

I made no secret of my political views, and Frank Allen

promptly dubbed me "the office Democrat," dramatizing my distinctly minority status in the newsroom. The atmosphere was mostly apolitical, however, and office politics was usually the only kind we talked about over a beer after the paper came out in late afternoon. In fact, I got on well with the leaders of both parties on those rare occasions when I had an opportunity to cover politics.

I managed to get a share of the *Courier*'s coverage of the 1938 campaign, helping out on both the governorship and the congressional races. It was heady stuff for a reporter only a few months out of college, but I was totally unprepared for the results: a debacle for the Democrats and a severe setback for Roosevelt's New Deal on November 8. As the trend became painfully clear on election night, I sat in stupefaction in the newsroom, unable to respond to the good-natured gibes from my Republican colleagues, who were astonished that I would take it so hard. I failed to offer even a mild demurrer during an election postmortem.

Most of my colleagues were suspicious of Roosevelt and believed the United States should remain aloof from Europe's problems. But with the threat of war mounting steadily, I only wanted Roosevelt to act and lead, at whatever political risk. Most of these friends tolerated me in good humor, and when Hitler fomented the Sudetenland crisis in Czechoslovakia that spring and summer, I noted more of them joining me after hours to hover over the Teletypes just off the newsroom to check on the latest developments. It's not that my newsroom colleagues were indifferent to international developments or uncaring about human misery in Spain, China, or anywhere else. It was simply that for me, at that moment in history, global issues offered stark choices between good and evil.

Shortly after arriving at the *Courier* I had chafed when assigned twice to interview two elderly Waterloo women who had made their first pilgrimages back to their native Germany and returned to paint the Third Reich in rosy hues. Neither woman could understand Americans' hostility toward Hitler. Another "local angle" story I covered was the first visit in many years to his hometown by Fred Kaltenbach, scion of a well-known Waterloo family, who was a Hitler glorifier and Nazi fanatic. He and his Nordic-type wife were received in friendly fashion by the Waterloo Rotary Club, where he made his all-out apologia for the Nazi regime and suggested that Rotarians might like to read his book, *Self-Determination, 1919.* I got a copy of the book, which had been his doctoral dissertation at a German university, and had to review it under deadline. I was lacking in the background imperative for delivering a balanced review. In embarrassment, I called up one of my former professors and kept him on the telephone half an hour examining Kaltenbach's points and having him explain what the Versailles Treaty was about. It was hardly my finest hour as a foreign affairs writer, though my professor was helpful and tolerant. Whenever I got in over my head, I always retreated to academia, and I've done that repeatedly in my career.

During my first year at the *Courier*—it would have been so on any newspaper of its particular regional character—I rarely got to cover any events that happened far from Waterloo. I knew there would never be a chance to cover World War II for the *Courier* (though later it used many of my INS dispatches from Africa and Europe). In fact, I saw no chance for advancement on the *Courier.* Jobs were tight, and none of the good journalists senior to me were disposed to move. So after two years, I got to INS headquarters in New York for an interview and soon was bound for Detroit and the wire-service job that would get me overseas as a war correspondent in May of 1942. I had never landed the prize beats on the *Waterloo Daily Courier,* but I had learned much from able colleagues and felt fortunate to have worked there.

Graham Hovey, who retired as director of the Michigan Journalism Fellows, is professor emeritus at the University of Michigan, where he teaches "New Challenges for U.S. Foreign Policy." He was a correspondent in World War II for International News Service, covering the German surrender in Africa, the liberation of Rome, the allied invasion of southern France, and the exploits of the French underground. Later, he was a foreign affairs reporter in Washington for the Associated Press and an assistant editor of the New Republic. *He served on the journalism faculties of the Universities of Minnesota and Wisconsin and held a Fulbright grant for two years in Italy, where he broadcast a weekly "Letter from Italy" for American public radio stations. Returning to newspaper work in 1956, he was editorial writer, United Nations correspondent, and European correspondent for the* Minneapolis Star-Tribune. *He joined the editorial board of* The New York Times *in 1965, then served that newspaper as a foreign affairs reporter in Washington before becoming director of Michigan's Journalism Fellows program.*

He won an Overseas Press Club of America award for "best press interpretation of foreign affairs" for United Nations coverage in 1958 and shared a National Headliners Club award that year. He received the Page One Award of the Newspaper Guild of the Twin Cities for a 1961 Minneapolis Tribune *series, "Report on Communist Europe." He is a recipient of the Outstanding Achievement Award for "Distinguished Service in Journalism" and the Alumni Achievement Award of the University of Northern Iowa.*

Hovey holds a bachelor's degree in journalism and a master's degree in political science from the University of Minnesota.

10

No Safety Net, No Shortcuts

 B E T S Y C A R T E R

"IwantobeajournalistinNewYork." For me it was always one word.

But there is no shortcut in any career, unless you're very lucky or you're born to it. You must do a lot of grunt work. I'm always attracted to people who are slightly off, who haven't gone to elite colleges, who don't have connections through their family and are doing it on their own. If you're lucky, you have some fun doing it.

Everything that you do, even if it seems really trivial, at some point lands back in your lap. As early as that first year, I learned not to say no to any assignment. By laying out type at *Air and Water News*, I learned how to balance a page. Then, when I was editor-in-chief of *New York Woman* and when I was at *Esquire*, I found I had a pretty good eye for design. In most cases, the point of first jobs is that you shouldn't stay longer than a year, especially if you're doing the same thing, day after day. If you're in it longer, it's probably too long. What's important is what you're learning.

On graduation day from the University of Michigan, I flew

from Ann Arbor to New York to be a journalist. I had worked during college as a waitress and baby-sitter to pay travel expenses. I had a degree in English, but I had no job and no money. I stayed for a month at various YWCAs. My first home in New York City was at the Y on Eleventh Avenue and Thirty-fourth Street, across from the old New Yorker Hotel. The area was overrun with prostitutes, and it was hairy, no place for a young graduate. I had huge debates with myself about whether I could afford to move to the uptown Y on Lexington Avenue, which I finally did. I would wake up in my little room, go to the Horn and Hardart automat for breakfast, and go out on interviews. However, being alone in New York never struck me as scary. I knew I wasn't going to be a secretary; I was going to hold out in order to do some sort of editorial job. I walked everywhere because I couldn't afford public transportation, and I walked in, just cold, to every publishing company in New York, including McGraw-Hill. The company had an opening and sent me to *Air and Water News*, one of several trade newsletters it published.

This was 1967, the year of the miniskirt. When I went to see Jim Marshall, the editor of *Air and Water News*, I wore a red plaid miniskirt, I mean really mini, with a red plaid jacket and white go-go boots. He was so kind to me. He hired me and months later said, "I gave you the job because anyone who had the nerve to show up the way you did would do anything." It had taken me close to a month to get that first job.

The offices were on Sixth Avenue and Fifty-second Street. *Air and Water News* was an eight-page weekly newsletter: "A weekly report on environmental problems, local, state, national and worldwide." It was sent to legislators, people in small agencies around the country, and companies developing such things as new exhaust systems for automobiles. Congress was passing legislation in the field, and the newsletter also followed every state, watching for new regulations. Few publications were writing about environmental topics then; *Air and Water News* was one of the first.

There were three of us: Jim, the editor-in-chief; Tom O'Donahue, the managing editor; and me. I was the editorial assistant. (Tom was the first person who ever told me about Janis Joplin. He'd gone to see her in concert and came back raving about her. I became a committed Janis Joplin fan.) I sat outside Jim's office and answered his phone: "Air and Water News." It took me years to stop saying it. I had to do some clerical tasks, like typing stories, but I was *not* a secretary. They let me report and write stories, and I helped paste up the newsletter. Every Friday, I would take it for printing to the McGraw-Hill Building on Forty-second Street, a beautiful art deco building.

My oldest friend and I had always planned to come to New York after college and share an apartment. I found an apartment on Eighty-eighth Street between Riverside Drive and West End Avenue. It cost about $300 a month. I couldn't afford it by myself, but I took it thinking that she would take it with me. The apartment was in the basement of a brownstone. It opened to a garden. I thought it was sweet. She came to see it with her mother, who said, "Absolutely not; you're not living here," and they walked away leaving me with exorbitant rent to pay. I went to Columbia University and put up signs saying that I needed a roommate. I got one who watched television incessantly; we didn't get along. I told her, "If you don't stop watching television, I'm going to kill you." Of course, I was just kidding.

Her brother, who was all of twenty-seven, called me up and said, "I hear you have threatened to kill my sister."

"Just metaphorically, " I said. "I wasn't really going to do it."

That was the year students at Columbia University rioted and took over the library. I was this working girl by day, and then after work I'd change into my hippie clothes and go to Columbia and protest. I was there every night for the entire spring. My roommate (Miss TV) was a student at Columbia, but she was on the "other side" and that caused a big rift between us. Nevertheless, we lived together for a year in this teeny one-bedroom apartment.

Every morning, I would get on the subway and get off at Fifty-second Street and Broadway and walk two blocks to the office. I thought the job was the coolest thing I'd ever done. Jim would make up a list of stories to do each week. I'd get press releases to rewrite and also get sent to events. We were on environmental mailing lists, and we would hear of a meeting on oil pollution, for example, and Jim would say, "Go cover it." We did pieces on lead poisoning and lead pollution. I spent a lot of time at noise pollution conferences, and at sewage treatment plants because water quality was a big issue. I liked going to the sewers. I liked wearing the thigh-high boots. I occasionally dated guys who worked at the sewage treatment plants. They always sent flowers.

At the end of the year, I had a collection of newsletters I had worked on, which were printed on pukey green paper that couldn't be duplicated by copier. I still have a notebook of the newsletters. Some of the headlines, which I also wrote, were: "Incinerators sealed with haste and optimism," "Citizens for clean Delaware air want compact," "California to enforce paint regulations," "Houston JC's plan '68 pollution show," and "Whispering pines may reveal pollution."

With a staff of just three people, so much had to be turned over so quickly that we didn't always have time to think about writing. I know my writing certainly needed calming down, cutting out adjectives, toning down the verbs. But I took the journalism part very seriously; subscribers were paying an enormous amount of money for this newsletter, and I had to get it right.

People I knew from school were applying for work at Condé

Nast magazines. One friend got a job at ABC. And here I was, on the same floor as people on the staff of *Chemical Engineering* magazine and weekly aviator magazines, far from the world of fashion periodicals, television, and newsmagazines. To some recent journalism graduates, it might have seemed a little peculiar where I was, but I didn't mind. I was happy to be doing what I was doing. At that point I wasn't imagining being at a big-name magazine. I was fantasizing about being a girl reporter, which I guess I was. Later, when I got to *Newsweek* and was a reporter, I never thought I wanted to do anything else. I was writing and reporting, and that seemed about as good as it gets.

One of my peak experiences that first year was being sent to a particular luncheon. (There were very few, if any, women at these events.) None of the guests knew beforehand what it was going to be about, and at the end of the meal the waiters scraped all the garbage off the plates at the table in full view of everyone. Then the sponsors introduced a machine—the first garbage compactor. As we left the luncheon, they gave us little briquettes of garbage. I was quite thrilled about the whole thing. I also went to a lunch where the sponsors showed what cigarette smoking does to your lungs. I actually saw how much tar is on lungs. It was so disgusting, I was impressed.

My greatest thrill that year was having two pieces picked up by the *Congressional Record.* One was an interview with Theodore Weiss, a New York congressman who had done a lot of work on noise pollution. The other was a piece I did myself on how pollution affects animals in the zoo.

I got the idea for the zoo story shortly after the lung lunch. I had visited the zoo and wondered, "If smoke pollution does what it does to humans, what does air pollution do to animals?" Apparently, no one had ever asked the question before. I told Jim my idea and he said, "Go knock yourself out." No one had studied the matter, but zookeepers had a lot to say about it. I reported it and found out that animals have the same respiratory ailments that humans do.

It was then that I realized that the joy of reporting is being able to ask any questions you want and to find out everything you ever wanted to know. That confirmed my childhood ambition. The only thing I wanted to do was to be a reporter. I also wanted to come up with a story that my sister, an artist, could illustrate. For the zoo piece, she drew three monkeys: one was gagging, one was blowing its nose, and one was wiping its eyes. I was so excited when the article was picked up and reprinted. My name was on it. Then I thought, "Who reads the *Congressional Record?*"

Although I had been thrown into something I obviously knew nothing about, that first year taught me that with reporting or digging, you can learn about any topic. I was surprisingly undaunted by the subject matter. It never occurred to me that I wouldn't get it. I was nervous in the beginning, but there was no reason to think I couldn't do it. When I went to *Esquire*, I was really scared. When I started *New York Woman* I was scared, and I was anxious when I went to *Harper's Bazaar*. But not then, not that first year.

A lot of reporting is about being fearless. I guess that coming to New York by myself, searching for a job and an apartment, having no money and getting through it gave me courage. I would ask sources anything. I would say anything. I was not shy. I didn't have a safety net. I had to support myself. Something happens when you assume you're on your own. There's no question but that you have to do it, because you're it. I think about that first year when I hire new people. I'm inevitably drawn to people who I think might have been, as I was, very plucky.

After a year at *Air and Water News* and another year at a trade magazine in Washington, D.C., I moved to Boston, job-hunting once again. I walked into the *Atlantic Monthly,* off the street, and said, "I must speak to the managing editor." She came downstairs and hired me on the spot. "The reason I'm hiring you is that you'll be me one day," she said. I didn't believe her for a second.

Betsy Carter is editor-in-chief of **New Woman.** *She helped launch* **Marie Claire** *and was executive editor at* **Harper's Bazaar.** *She started* **New York Woman** *in 1986 and was its editor-in-chief until it folded in the winter of 1992. Before that, she was editorial director at* **Esquire,** *and for nine years a reporter and writer at* **Newsweek,** *where she applied after working nearly a year at the* **Atlantic Monthly** *in Boston. She also worked at the* **Shield,** *a bank trade magazine in Washington, D.C. Carter holds a bachelor's degree in English from the University of Michigan.*

11

The Case of the Missing Lids

 PAM LUECKE

School officials at Northwestern University, where I was finishing graduate school, recommended that we blanket our region of choice with résumés—then accept any job that had to do with words. This was 1975, right after Watergate and Nixon's fall, and jobs were tight. I was engaged to my college sweetheart, who was from Massachusetts, and I decided to flood New England with letters. I set up various appointments with anyone who would see me and started a job-hunting tour with all my worldly possessions in the back of my silver Toyota station wagon. One of the first places I stopped was the *The Hartford Courant*, where the lifestyle editor had an opening. She interviewed me, and the newspaper offered me a job as a "lifestyle reporter," a title bigger than the job itself. But it had to do with words.

The walls of the department were painted bright yellow. It stood out from the rest of the newspaper office, which was dingy and cluttered. The editor was Betty Barrett, who was about sixty years old. She was the classic early-woman-in-journalism. She had never married, seemed to have worked at the *Courant* forever, and was trying to bring the women's pages into the 1970s.

The department had recently become the lifestyle department in name, but in practice it still produced the traditional women's page. There were seven or eight of us in the department, and we were involved in covering food, fashion, women's clubs, weddings and engagements, and "lifestyle," a concept that was still being defined. Everyone in the department except for one copy editor was female. The section was a magnet for incredible calls from the public: "I'm in the middle of making a soufflé, and it flopped; what should I do?" "What am I going to wear to a wedding in April? Is it too early to wear white shoes?" We were stunned that the public would call this group of mostly twenty-three-year-old women and ask us such questions. Of course, we didn't have a clue. But they were calling the women's section of the newspaper because they thought we were authorities, so we tried to help.

Half my job—and I knew this going in—was handling weddings and engagements. The paper had standardized forms that we sent to prospective brides. When the forms came in, I typed up little write-ups for the section. I called the family if I had a question and scheduled the announcement for publication, making sure the right ones got in the paper on the right Sunday and didn't get in before the event. The wedding beat forced me to stay organized. I cropped pictures using grease pencils and a sizing wheel. We wouldn't use the picture of the bridegroom—for no real reason, except space—so we'd crop him out if someone had submitted a photo of the couple. I had a lot of heated discussions with brides about that. I also had to read page proofs carefully to make sure the composing room hadn't put the wrong photograph with an announcement. I learned how to work with compositors to make a page layout come out even, how to count characters in a headline to make it fit, how to send through corrections. I learned how the paper was produced.

You have to get names right when you're doing weddings and engagements. Hell hath no fury like the mother of a bride when her daughter's name has been misspelled. My husband, George Graves, also a journalist, got hired right after college, and he started by taking obituaries over the phone. We laugh about these first-year assignments now, but we both learned a very healthy respect for spelling people's names correctly.

There were peak seasons in weddings and engagements. Valentine's Day was big, as was June and August and Christmas. During those times I worked on announcements every day; at other times it was less frequent. Since this assignment was only half my job, I viewed it as what I had to do so I could do stories. Eventually I shed my wedding and engagement duties and became a full-time reporter. But even in that first year, I had a lot of freedom and autonomy. I could pursue any story that caught my fancy, such as a new program at a social service agency or a new recreational fad. One early story was a first-person account of life at the YWCA, where I had lived for a month or two when I first arrived in town. The Y board was not very happy about my account, which was not flattering, and called the managing editor to complain. I was very relieved that he backed me up. As I learned more about how the world worked and how journalism worked, I gradually began to do a little less fluff. I wrote a story that year on the tenth anniversary of *Griswold* v. *Connecticut*. The court ruling, which legalized birth control in the state by recognizing the right to privacy, became a fundamental underpinning of *Roe* v. *Wade*.

We also interviewed visiting celebrities or experts. A fashion model or author came to town, and I interviewed him or her. These are the people that you now hear on radio and TV talk shows. I learned then that these stories are rarely worth doing.

They don't make particularly good copy because the people are usually on a book tour or promotional tour and have been asked all the same questions a million times before.

The big push for our department was the Sunday lifestyle section, which had a cover, and its own front page. The rest of the week our stories were stuck inside the A-section or the B-section. We geared our thoughts and energies for the Sunday cover. The paper was experimenting with color photography in our Sunday sections, and we had to coordinate closely with the photo staff. We would ask the people being photographed to wear bright, solid colors—no prints or plaids—which would have been disastrous if the reproduction was off-register.

I loved setting up interviews and going out and meeting people. I thought this was the neatest thing in the world and couldn't believe they were paying me to do it. Journalism school had prepared me, and I had already gotten over my stage fright. At Northwestern, the professors turned you loose in Chicago and said, "Call up somebody and get there, somehow, on public transportation and interview them." When I was in Connecticut and called people up, they were thrilled that a reporter, and not a student, was coming to talk to them. I had a car and became familiar with the state and parts of New England. Once I drove to the Greenwich Country Club, an hour and a half away, where I was to interview a man who supposedly had invented racquetball. (It was just catching on as a sport.) I'd never been to Greenwich before but knew it was supposed to be very hoity-toity. The muffler on my car fell off on the way there, and I drove into the country club sounding like a percussionist. I was quite embarrassed but had to carry on.

That year I had my first page-one story. Although commonplace now, it was unheard of for anyone writing for lifestyle pages to write for the main part of the newspaper. But here was legitimate news: Homemakers were ready to put up vegetables, and they couldn't because there was a shortage of canning-jar lids in Connecticut and nationwide. No one was quite sure of the reason, but the shortage prompted hoarding and panic-buying. After writing about the shortage for the front page, I discovered that a lid manufacturer was located in Connecticut; I toured the factory and used the information I gathered as the basis for a follow-up story for the lifestyle section. I was so proud. This was the beginning of my interest in business journalism.

One of the things I learned from my editor, who could be very crusty, was how to interact with the public and how to say no. She knew what she wanted and what she didn't want, and she didn't hesitate to tell people that. For example, she had implemented a democratic wedding page where everybody's picture was the same size. In the old days if you were somewhat prominent, or were someone the editor liked, you would get a big picture and a headline, while someone else wouldn't get her picture in at all. Although Betty was adamant, women still would come in, furious because they didn't get a bigger picture or headline. She didn't have a private office. We were all in an open room. Nothing much was carried on in private, and I learned from other people's telephone styles. I learned from her how to say no to mothers of the bride, and to those, for instance, who tried to get us to do a Sunday cover story about an upcoming charity ball.

In the first year, I also learned the discrepancy between what journalists think a newspaper is for and what the public thinks it's for. I can still remember getting into arguments with what we'd refer to as club ladies. They would call and want us to print their press release, and we would ask, "Is the event open to the public?" They would say no.

"We don't see any reason to put it in the paper," we'd say.

"But we want it for our scrapbook," they'd respond.

Betty was trying to change the pages from the old days—when the women's auxiliaries and clubs ran the section—into a newsier section where the editor and reporters identified trends and issues that affected the way people live. I admire Betty a lot for starting the process. But she had to deal with both the public—the people who were traditionally the readers and beneficiaries of the old style—and the realities inside the paper. The reality inside was that it was still a section that very few men would consider working for. Diversity was not a concept then. We were all white. We were young. We were women. We were viewed very much as second-class citizens within the newspaper.

Consequently, I was somewhat in awe of the reporters in the newsroom because they were "real reporters," out covering exotic zoning committees. My career went from working in features, which is one niche, to business, which is another. It wasn't until I became regional editor that I got into mainline journalism, and I'm aware of gaps in my background. I was never a local news reporter. I was involved later in covering the state general assembly as a business writer, but I wish that I'd had more of a reporting background in general news, because it's different coming to it as an editor.

I remember going to a party where I knew there would be "real reporters" and making a point the week before to read their stories very carefully so I would have something to talk about. I wanted to make sure I could hold my ground. It was my goal to get into the newsroom. But at the same time, I thought I was so lucky just to have a job in journalism with a major newspaper. Some of my classmates had started with trade publications or with newspapers that had a circulation of 15,000. I was at a big-city paper, and I had regular hours.

During that first year, I decided to get my M.B.A. and started attending night classes the following fall. In the course of my studies, I also became interested in business as a subject to write about. Had I had a hard news job, with its irregular, unpredictable hours, I might never have gone to business school. As with the front-page canning-lid story, I found I could put a business spin on my lifestyle stories. I started reading *The Wall Street Journal,* and I learned how to spot a trend. We used to joke that if you found three examples of a phenomenon, or if you found something rising or declining—disco dancing or milkmen—that was a trend. It was what the lifestyle section looked for.

I had gone to business school for a couple of reasons. Friends from Northwestern who were getting their M.B.A.s were being counseled to hold out for jobs that would pay them at least $15,000 a year. "Wow, they're making a lot of money," I thought. Journalists were being counseled to grab anything that offered $7,000. I had also realized that the newspaper would often take people who were good reporters—but knew nothing about managing—and promote them to be editors. I went to business school with the idea of someday becoming an editor, thinking that if I wanted to get into newspaper management, it would be good for me to know something about it. But I learned a lot from Betty, too, especially what it takes to change an organization.

Pam Luecke is assistant managing editor of the metro department at The Hartford Courant, *where she supervises the politics and government staff, statewide specialists, and special projects reporters. She left Hartford in 1979 and worked in Louisville at* The Courier-Journal *and* Louisville Times *as business reporter, business editor, and regional editor before returning to Hartford in 1989. She has supervised coverage of Pulitzer Prize–winning articles at both the* Courier-Journal *and* The Courant. *She was a Bagehot Fellow at Colum-*

bia University. She holds a bachelor's degree in philosophy from Carleton College in Northfield, Minnesota, a master's degree in journalism from Northwestern University, and an M.B.A. from the University of Hartford. She was also a visiting journalism professor at the University of Connecticut.

12

Trust Your Instincts

 MIREYA NAVARRO

A teachers' strike was scheduled for the morning after I began at the *San Francisco Examiner*. My first assignment was to talk to parents about what they would do when striking teachers shut down one of the largest public school systems in the country, keeping thousands of kids from school. Many parents would need to find day care and make other arrangements for their children. My editor, knowing I was new, said to me, "Why don't you call the parents' association and start from there, and ask them to find parents you can talk to."

The parents' association said it would help. "But first we have to call parents and then have them call you," I was told. "Because of confidentiality reasons, we can't just release the names." So I sat by the phone while these people did my legwork. An hour and a half went by, and I hadn't gotten a single call. I knew that something was wrong, and I told the reporter who sat next to me what was happening. "Listen," he said. "Why don't you just go to Macy's department store, which is a few blocks away, and any shoppers with kids are bound to have kids in public school." Sure enough, I walked the few blocks to Macy's and went to the toy department, and there were plenty of parents with kids. I interviewed a lot of them right on the spot. It took me less than an hour to go back with a story. And it showed me that I had to trust my own instincts. What an editor said was not necessarily gospel. Next time I would listen to an editor's instruction but also find other ways to get a story, to report it and write it. It was a lesson that served me well, particularly as a beat reporter who constantly has to rely on her own initiative.

After getting my journalism degree in 1979 from George Washington University, I went through a summer program at the University of California at Berkeley run by the Institute for Journalism Education. The program trained minorities to work in newspapers, increasing their numbers in newsrooms. Instead of returning home to Puerto Rico, I interviewed with the *Dallas Times Herald* (which has since gone out of business) and the *San Francisco Examiner.* The *Examiner* hired me.

I didn't know anybody in San Francisco. I had no single friend or relative there. Everybody in the newsroom was much older. I lived to work and spent my first year working long hours. Twelve-hour days were not uncommon. I had done very few stories beforehand and was very tentative when I began. During my first few weeks, I covered press conferences and demonstrations, court hearings and political election campaigns, learning on the job. One campaign produces many stories, and I discovered how to follow a campaign until the election. In court I learned the difference between a preliminary hearing and an arraignment, when the defendant enters a plea, and other steps leading to a trial. In writing about trials, I learned that the proper terminology was opening "statement" and closing "argument."

Working for an afternoon paper that is the underdog in the

market (the *Examiner* had fewer readers than the *San Francisco Chronicle*), we felt the push to find the scoop or get the story first. We don't have the circulation, we were told, but we could be the better paper. A woman in Alameda County had been arrested for stealing. Her defense was that she suffered from multiple personalities and that one of the other personalities was active during the crime. After the arrest, my editors sent me to find her. They really wanted an interview with this woman. She was a mother, lived in a middle-class neighborhood, and had no criminal record. Why was this woman stealing?

I went to her home, which was a half hour from my bureau. I knocked on the door, and she answered. I tried to get her to talk, and she kept saying, "My lawyer told me not to talk to a reporter." I could tell that she wanted to talk. I tried very nicely, because I'm not the kind of person to push too much. Once it was obvious that she wouldn't budge, I left. I said to myself, "Oh, my God. What am I going to tell my editors? I talked to the woman. I actually saw her. I could have touched her, and I couldn't get the interview."

I went to my car and locked it, deliberately leaving the keys inside. I went back to the house, told her my troubles with the car, and asked if I could please use her phone. I called the desk and said I had locked myself out of my car and asked if someone could pick me up. It wasn't that easy, I was told. The woman overheard the conversation and offered me a ride.

During the ride she started talking. I couldn't take notes because that would have made her nervous. But I agreed that I would check with her attorney and would leave out anything he thought would hurt her case. I listened intently and etched a few things in my mind. She just talked and talked and talked. At this point, all I wanted was a few quotes from the woman, and I made a point of remembering three direct quotes. She explained that most times she was a decent, law-abiding mother, but suddenly she could become a totally different person, one who could steal, lie, and cheat. I believed her. She seemed to be suffering from this multiple-personality syndrome. She dropped me off at the office, and I called her attorney.

"Nothing she said made her look bad," I said, telling him what we had talked about. "In fact, I think people would be sympathetic." He was swayed and said okay. The next day I had a front-page story that no one else had.

I don't know if I would ever be as willing to lock myself out of my car again. I would probably be less impulsive and think about the consequences. The plan could have backfired. She could have just told me to get lost, and I'd be a half hour away from the bureau, and how would I get back? But this is why editors love young, hungry reporters.

During that year, I worked first in the city newsroom, then was transferred to the Alameda County bureau, and before the year was up I asked my editor to transfer me back to the city. I was very disappointed in the bureau because the emphasis was on quantity. There was little time to research and write longer pieces or to spend time digging up stories. Even the story about the woman with the personality disorder was done quickly. I almost considered leaving journalism because I didn't feel that what I wrote was worthwhile.

Part of the reason is that I'm not a fast writer. To this day, I overreport stories. I feel that I need some expertise in a subject before I can write about it. I'm very nitpicky. I want to know everything before I write. Some reporters are good at writing every day and working under deadline pressure. They love that; they thrive on that. It just made me miserable. My ideal job is the one I have now at *The New York Times*. I spend days, if not weeks, on stories that would never run if I had not spent that much time on them. They require a lot of interviewing and investigation, and I enjoy that much more.

I didn't have that luxury my first year. One Sunday I showed up for work, and the editors said I had to cover the gay and lesbian parade in downtown San Francisco. It was panic time. I never had covered a story that involved hundreds and thousands of people. I wasn't prepared, and I had no idea of the magnitude of the event. I went to the assignment thinking it would be a parade of a few hundred people, and I couldn't believe the numbers of people, not only the contingent of those participating but the bystanders. People had gotten up early just to stake out a place. You could look up Market Street, San Francisco's downtown street, and see miles of people. It was a festive mood; people were dancing and clapping. It reminded me of Mardi Gras in New Orleans or Carnival in Rio. For a moment I didn't know where to begin. I didn't know what to do.

I first narrowed my tasks to finding out—among all those thousands of people—who was in charge. There were monitors all along the parade route, and I started asking questions, such as who was handling the press. With more experience, and knowing what the assignment was, I would have tried to figure this out before the day of the parade. But I was sent with no previous notice. I did find someone with press kits, which took care of nuts-and-bolts information, the theme of the parade, who was participating. Then I went through a few basic steps in my mind: talk to the marchers, talk to the onlookers, write some descriptions of the scene. I took a deep breath and started going through my list as though I were going through a recipe, doing one thing and then the other. Otherwise I would have been totally overwhelmed. It was one of those experiences that make you think, "I'm here, but I don't know what I'm doing." Eventually I covered three of those parades and wasn't even worried about the basics, but the first one I was just happy to report and get the story out.

During the summer program at Berkeley, I had learned that you take quotes verbatim, and you don't put something in a quote that you're not certain about, even if it's one preposition. But when you're covering something in real life and writing in your note-book, you tend to come up with your own shorthand. Joan Baez had just come back from Southeast Asia, and I went to interview her about her work with refugees. I was taking notes and quoting her, and she said, "Indochina." I wrote down "I," thinking I would remember later what it stood for. I wrote the story and translated the "I" as "Indonesia," which appeared in the paper the next day. There are certain things you just don't pick up until you read history the next day. I was so embarrassed. She didn't call to de-mand a correction, but it always mortified me that I had made such a stupid mistake. From then on, I never abbreviated proper names. I can't trust my memory. And editors may not pick up on an error.

That first year, I read the paper every day and had my favorite writers. I picked out people I thought I should emulate. I looked for clear, explanatory writing. I particularly liked wit in stories, and I looked for clever story ideas that were obviously a reporter's. I could tell because a reporter who had covered breaking news would write a feature off the news a day or so later. By reading their stories, I learned how to see beyond the story I was covering for the next day. One of the reporters I really liked covered the 1980 Census, an assignment that turned into a year's worth of stories about how the census was prepared. Her stories were on the front page all the time. She found new ways to focus the story, writing about the census from the point of view of the census taker, for example. She would spend a day with census takers and create a human interest story about the tedious work of trying to find people to count.

That particular reporter's work stood in my mind ten years later, shortly after I joined the *Times*, when I realized the 1990 Census was about to occur. I decided to take my metro editor out to lunch. "Listen," I said, "next year is the 1990 Census, and if you don't have anyone in mind, I'd like to cover that story for the year." The metro department had not even planned for it because it was months away and the *Times* was covering it as a national story from Washington. It wasn't one of the things the metro editor was thinking about. Fortunately he said, "Sure. Go ahead."

I basically appropriated the beat, writing human interest stories about people who did not want to be counted, immigrants who were here illegally, homeless people. The stories played very well in the paper. Had it not been for the exposure to this great reporter during my first year, I wouldn't have thought about covering it. The census is not what you die to cover unless you have some strategy. I credit that coverage with positioning me in the *Times* newsroom as someone who could be trusted with a beat. And the next time I asked for a beat, on AIDS, I got it right away.

One of the first longer pieces I did that year was a story about low riders. This was a Hispanic phenomenon. Guys would customize old American cars, repairing and repainting them. They put hydraulic systems in the car to make it ride a few inches above the pavement and jump up and down. I was totally fascinated by that. I had never seen it before. I checked the newspaper library to see if the *Examiner* had ever done any stories on low riders, and the librarian couldn't find any clips. So I said, "I'll do a big story on them."

I did a main story on the drivers—who they were, their favorite cruising spots, and why these guys, who were not well-to-do, spent every bit of money, every single cent they had, on their cars. They said they took great satisfaction in taking a piece of junk and working on it until it became a museum piece. They were artists. They would say things like, "I love my car better than my girl-friend" in front of the girlfriend—who would understand. I also wrote a sidebar about riding along with one of them. During the ride, people just stared. The driver was thrilled "hopping" the car, getting it to move up and down like a rodeo horse. He was a peacock spreading his feathers. I always felt that because I was not from San Francisco and because I was such a rookie and every-thing surprised and amazed me, I paid attention to a story that had been playing out in front of everyone's eyes for years. Yet no one had been interested in covering it. I guess this stems from my being in a new place and looking at everything through fresh eyes.

The low-rider stories also showed why it's good to have some-one in the newsroom who is Hispanic and speaks Spanish. The phenomenon was confined to a Hispanic neighborhood, but I think a paper has a responsibility to find stories wherever they are. I never set out to cover just Hispanics or to cover only my com-munity. Yet by virtue of my language skills I could do stories that other reporters were not doing.

I'm definitely for more representation of minorities in the news-room, especially in a city like New York. You need a variety of reporters with different language skills, because that's what the city is. Diversity in the newsroom will serve a paper because it will reflect the interest of the community. The best way to cover any minority community, though, is to incorporate it into mainstream stories. Rather than doing a story that's happening to Latinos, or happening to blacks, you just make sure that the story you write has representation from those groups. A lot of the problems that affect these communities affect everyone. That's the way it works in the real world.

Since 1989 Mireya Navarro has been a staff writer at The
New York Times, *where she writes about AIDS. She spent
ten years with the* San Francisco Examiner, *reporting on
courts, consumer affairs, and general assignments. She covered
foreign assignments in Central America and Mexico City. She
is an adjunct professor at Columbia Journalism School, teaching reporting and writing, was a University of Michigan Journalism Fellow, and holds a bachelor's degree in journalism
from George Washington University.*

13

Stabbings and Sacred Cows

 STEPHEN L. PETRANEK

When I got to the *Democrat and Chronicle*, a 125,000-circulation daily in Rochester, New York, I had a rude awakening. Overnight, I had descended from the heights of journalism to the bottom of the heap. As editor-in-chief of my college daily, *The Diamondback*, at the University of Maryland, I had already run a newspaper with a paid staff of more than one hundred. And just before I took the job in Rochester I had run my own news syndicate from Europe, which I set up for my master's project at the University of Missouri. I had signed up newspapers in the states, then gone to Brussels to write for them about the emerging Common Market. It was heady stuff. Almost all the papers printed everything I wrote. And there were genuine scoops. I had written about the Chunnel, the new tunnel under the English Channel, long before anyone in the states had heard of it. I wrote about the miracle of Holland's polders, thousands of acres reclaimed from the sea with dikes and run as perfect little socialist communities. I was so confident, striding into the *Democrat and Chronicle* that first day in the spring of 1971, I speculated I already had more and better clips than some of the reporters who had been there several years.

Within hours, my oh-so-solid ego was shattered. Suddenly, I was a cub reporter, a nobody, the new guy, lowest of the low. That was tough. Furthermore, I happened into that newsroom in the middle of a major overhaul of American newspapers—around the country newspapers were ridding themselves of the old self-trained fire-engine chasers and were hiring bright kids fresh out of journalism schools. College graduates were replacing the green eyeshade crowd, and the latter didn't take kindly to know-it-alls like me. The old guys knew what they were doing. There was no doubt about that. They had fantastic skills and intuition, and they made the competition so thick you could breathe it, maybe even choke on it. Everyone at the paper seemed to view me with skepticism, if not outright suspicion.

The old guard controlled the system, which made things difficult for newcomers: They knew the city, and they knew the sources. They had the best beats locked up. If a new person wanted to make a mark, which meant getting on the front page, he or she would have to take chances. The story had to be written with flair and imagination, or it had to have such astounding facts that the words didn't matter. Writing with flair meant a higher rate of failure—unreliable deadline writers were not needed.

My first job was writing obituaries. I hated writing obits. There were two approaches you could take—read old clips from the morgue, piecing together the essential accomplishments of the person's life bolstered by a bio from the funeral home, or—if you could do it—call the family. Early on I figured out that a good obit was nothing more than a good profile, except that the subject was dead. That meant doing something few at the *Democrat* had tried to do—using quotes and anecdotes, building scenes, capturing emotional rather than factual events. But there are few things in journalism harder than talking to the spouse of someone who has died the day before.

I remember my first obit. It was about twenty column inches long; most obits were about four column inches. I finished it and gave it to Jerry Ceppos, the city editor. He and I were close friends. He had been the editor-in-chief of *The Diamondback* two years before me. He liked my spirit, he said. But he also liked short obits, so more of them could run. I sat at my desk, pretending to type, watching as he slashed the obit in half, shaking his head. The copy chief, who sat in the center of a semicircular desk—just like the ones they describe in journalism school—looked at what remained of the obit and went nuts. He strode over to talk to Jerry. Then he went back to the copy editors. They huddled, shaking their heads, muttering something like, "This isn't the way we do things here," but they put it through. All the while, I managed to give the appearance of typing away.

One man I had to do an obit on had never been written about before. He had no children, and his only living relative was his wife. He was in his sixties and he seemed unremarkable, the sort of guy who went to work every day at Eastman Kodak, like thousands of other people in Rochester. He had a fairly respectable research job but never invented anything. There was nothing to do but dig. It turned out, unraveling the threads of his life, that he had been an amazing contributor, both in time and money, to charities. He was always doing things for other people, taking in some kid rather than see him go off to a foster home, constantly and selflessly giving of himself. The obit ended up a full-fledged story on the front page of the city section.

In a short time, I discovered that almost anyone's life could make an interesting story if I dug enough. But it was like being an oncologist; I had to ignore the circumstances in order to do the job. My goal was to produce stories, stories good enough to get me off obits. The only way I was going to produce good stories was to keep talking to unhappy people.

The city desk consisted of four desks pushed together for the city editor and three assistant city editors. They were the center of the universe. As the obit person, my desk didn't quite touch theirs, as if to make sure everyone understood I was in their control but an outcast too. When I wasn't writing obits, which took priority, the editors would give me stories to rewrite. I'd write a lead or fix a paragraph. No matter what I thought of what was handed to me, I accepted it enthusiastically and kept my mouth shut. I was thrilled to be working in a real newsroom. I was probably the happiest, most cooperative obit writer they ever had. Inside, though, I sometimes worried that I was making a terrible mistake. The editors liked me doing obits and rewrite. Was I cooperating too much? Was I going to spend my whole life doing this? A day feels like a lifetime when you're just starting out, and it wasn't long before my impatience got the best of me and I started asking, "How long will I be doing this?" No one had an answer. What I was looking for was some security, someone to say, "You do this for six months, then we give you something else." I kept asking. It wasn't long before I learned my first lesson in being careful about what I wished for.

One night I came in to work and the police reporter was sick. "You're going over to do cops," the editor said.

Typically, a reporter would not go into something like the police beat cold. You would always be led over to the police station by someone who would show you the ropes, spend a few nights with you, and introduce you around. "I have no idea what to do," I said.

"You'll figure it out," the editor said, dismissing me. Very alone, I walked across the street to the police station where a room was set aside for the *Democrat and Chronicle* reporter. The desk was empty except for a couple of pencils, a typewriter that looked as if it had been through seven wars, a phone, and a wire basket that contained police reports. Nothing else was in the room, no carpet, no shades, no window. I'd never seen a police report in my life. I sat at the desk, shuffling through the basket, listening to the police radio, which was just outside the room on the dispatcher's desk. I sat that way for three or four hours. Every hour or so someone would call from the desk: "Anything happening?"

"Huh?" I said.

"We need your stories," the editor on the other end of the line said.

"Stories? What stories?"

I was supposed to have taken the most interesting police reports—car thefts, break-ins, whatever—and written them up as fillers. I did four stories in twenty minutes.

The next day, I was back at obits. After about three months I was assigned to the police beat full-time. I should have been happy, but I soon found out that cops, which was jargon for police beat, was even worse than obits. And I asked again, "How long will I be doing this?" and again no one answered.

I took the same approach with police reports as I had with obits. If I found something interesting, I'd ask for more information. The cops who filled out those reports didn't put much effort into them, so many reports were unintelligible. But one night when a dead body was discovered, I sensed something funny about the report. I got the dispatcher to get me in touch with the cop who had written it. Gradually, I pulled the story out of him. A body had been found in the trunk of a car owned by a respectable person in a respectable neighborhood. The policeman wouldn't tell me the cause of death, but he sort of whispered, "Call the coroner; there was a hole right through the guy's head." I turned that report into a story that got a lot of play.

Some nights I'd come in, and there would be no police reports in the wire basket. Panic—those reports were my only leads. Without them, I couldn't produce the stories I had to produce. I'd go over to the complaint desk and ask, "Where are the police reports?" If the person working the complaint desk had any excuse at all, it would be something like, "No one got around to Xeroxing them today." After a while, I made friends with the night dispatcher, and she allowed me to make my own copies.

If anything happened, like a fire, I went to the scene. I prayed for fires—any kind of action—but most nights nothing happened. I was like a prisoner in an isolation cell. I never saw my friends in the newsroom, never saw the outside of that police station. My name was in the paper less than when I was doing obits. After what seemed like weeks, something broke. There was a major disturbance in one of the poorest sections in the city. I jumped in the car and drove into the neighborhood. People were rioting. There was looting of buildings, glass being broken. I was driving down one street, heading toward a police cruiser to talk to the cop, when all of a sudden the back window of the car I was driving was broken by a bottle or rock. Within seconds, it seemed as if every piece of glass in the car was knocked out. I couldn't see a thing. I was terrified, and I got out of there fast. I stuck my head out the driver's window, put my foot to the floor, and drove to the police station. Still shaking, I got the dispatcher to hook me up with the cops at the scene, and I interviewed them over the police radio.

The cops treated police reporters like a necessary annoyance. They were not happy to talk to me. They were not happy to have me in their building. It was a difficult place to work, but it was where I got my early and best breaks.

One night a garbled, brief, difficult-to-understand message came across the police radio about a stabbing at Midtown Mall, the new mall built in the middle of the city, which was a point of great civic pride in Rochester. This was a successful, upwardly mobile town where there were not a lot of poor people and it had a clear sense of itself. It's the place where George Eastman grew up and founded Eastman Kodak; it's the birthplace of the Xerox Corporation, the birthplace of Sybron, Bausch and Lomb, and a number of nationally prominent corporations.

The idea of a stabbing at this new mall was antithetical to everything the town stood for. This was a prestigious place, not the kind of place to get sullied by violence. My normal procedure after hearing the radio would have been to check with the city desk before leaving my post to make sure everyone agreed I should leave. This time I didn't even think about procedure. I just ran, down several flights of stairs, as hard as I could, to midtown, a few blocks away. I was breathless when I got there, but I got there so quickly that even though the person who had been stabbed had already been taken away, I found a few eyewitnesses. After interviewing them, then the cops, I reconstructed the scene. The story ran stripped across the front page. I got a note from the executive editor and a memo from the publisher. It was a turning point.

Before that story, reporters at the paper hadn't taken me seriously. Because I worked out of the police station instead of the newsroom, I wasn't developing relationships with other writers. The Midtown Mall story changed everything. I started getting invited to the bar where the reporters hung out, started getting invited to social events. When I went into the office to get assignments, people came up to me and talked to me. Even the managing editor remembered my name. All because of one piece.

I learned a lot from one guy, who was sort of a career assistant city editor. His name was Ted Case. He was a real pro, a good-natured guy with a gruff exterior. He'd hand me back a story and say, "It's all screwed up." Then he'd carefully explain what I needed to do to fix it.

"This is an editorial," he said flatly of one article I had written.

"What do you mean, 'This is an editorial'?" I asked.

"It's full of your own opinion and unsubstantiated fact, and you'll have to prove to me how you know this stuff," he replied.

I thought what I had written was the sort of information you could take for granted, but I soon learned to nail down every fact and attribute everything. One night I came back from the police station just before two in the morning and heard something about a murder on the police radio. The editors asked me to check it out. We had an absolute deadline of two o'clock, after which you could not get another piece of type in the paper, but somehow I got enough information in a few minutes to know that a man had been killed in the parking lot of a nightclub. My source was the owner of the nightclub where the murder had taken place. But I couldn't get confirmation from the cops. The editors chose not to run the story, which meant that our afternoon competition would get it. Another lesson learned. I had killed myself trying to make that deadline. But no confirmation, no story.

Later that first year, I began covering suburban towns. This felt like going from the war zone to a peaceful atoll in the South Pacific. I covered school board meetings, local politics, things that people care about in their everyday lives. Things that I had no interest in whatsoever. I had never paid property taxes, never owned a home. I couldn't identify with the concerns of my own readers. Because people in one suburb didn't care about what was going on in the others, fiefdom stories rarely ran the whole press-run. It wasn't a good way to get on the front page.

Finally, I found a way to make noise—confront a sacred cow. About thirty miles outside the city of Rochester is one of the first nuclear power plants: the R. E. Ginna Nuclear Power Plant, operated by Rochester Gas and Electric. I was covering the eastern suburbs, which extended to the boundary of the plant. Some of the people in those communities were concerned about safety. They wanted the utility company to install monitors to check for radiation. I called RG&E and said, "Send me everything you've got." The company did, including a quarterly report that goes to stockholders.

I read in the report that the plant recently had been shut down for several months of maintenance. This plant comprised about one-third of the capability of the entire electrical network, and I thought, "How in the world can a power company afford a generating station that shuts down that long?" I went to one of the assistant city editors and said, "There's something funny about this. I want to take some time to look into this." They weren't normally inclined to allow me to spend time reporting something that might not produce a story for the next day. My leash was short.

"Take a couple of hours," the editor said.

I called the gas and electric company and was informed that the plant had been shut down because the fuel rods had to be replaced. I said, "How often do you have to do this?" The response: "Not very often."

"How often?" I repeated. As soon as I heard "We have to get back to you on that," I knew something was up. The next day, I had the metro section lead about the plant being shut down. But I still had a lot of unanswered questions. My editors let me work on it a little longer, until the questions were answered. But I kept coming up with more questions that the company had to get back to me on. When I couldn't get good answers from Rochester Gas and Electric, I contacted the nuclear regulatory agency, which sent me tons of boring documents that were written for engineers. Finally, all those hours in college science labs paid off. From the reports, I was able to figure out that problems had cropped up in other plants built by the same company.

Strangely, it turned out to be more of a super business story than a health story. Rochester was a town built on profits in the stock market from all those incredible growth companies. A single share of the Haloid Company purchased in the late 1940s was worth a small fortune in Xerox stock by the 1970s. People in Rochester cared less about the dangers of meltdown and more about what it meant to their RG&E stock.

The story of the Ginna Nuclear Power Plant became a major investigative series that spilled into my second year at the paper. The editors yanked me off covering the suburbs. It seemed to take forever to get to that point—a whole year—but it was one of the most invigorating and exciting years of my career. Finally, I had become a newsroom regular.

Stephen L. Petranek is a senior editor at Life *magazine. While at the* Democrat and Chronicle *he was an investigative reporter and consumer writer and won the John Hancock Award for financial reporting before becoming editor of the newspaper's Sunday magazine. He was also editor of Sunday magazines at* The Miami Herald *and* The Washington Post, *where he worked for thirteen years before moving to* Life. *He holds a bachelor's degree in journalism from the University of Maryland and a master's degree in journalism from the University of Missouri.*

14

Ducks Versus Geese

 D A V E   B A R R Y

I guess I didn't harm the *Daily Local News* too much; it's still there. After getting my degree in English from Haverford College in 1969, I did two years of alternative service work as a conscientious objector working in New York as a bookkeeper for the national headquarters of the Episcopal Church and then went to Philadelphia looking for a job. Friends knew an editor at the *Daily Local News* in West Chester, Pennsylvania, a suburb of Philadelphia. I went in, and miraculously, the paper was looking for three entry-level reporters. I don't think a paper of that size would hire anyone cold today. But it took a chance with me. (I had written columns for my high school and college papers, but my only real experience was as a summer intern at the *Congressional Quarterly*, where I would pick up copies of testimony on Capitol Hill for the real reporters.)

I started as a basic general assignment reporter. In the morning I came in and had certain things to do: Some days I'd take obituaries from funeral directors. I would call the fire departments checking for whose garage burned down. Once I had to cover a fire.

This was a small town, and fires were the big story. I spent a lot of time getting details from the fire officials. I even had quotes from some guy watching his house burn down. He gave me his name, but I didn't bother to ask, "Do you spell Smith with an 'i'?" (He didn't.) You learn to ask. You don't assume anything.

What I was learning was real basic, such as calling up people who don't want to talk to you. I didn't know anything about journalism. I was a pretty good writer, and I thought that was all that mattered. I was more of a writer than a journalist. But journalism isn't about writing. You learned that what it's really about is asking hard questions, being persistent. I learned about journalism from listening to other reporters, from not assuming things, and from realizing that you do not avoid asking a question just because you think you know the answer or it is embarrassing to ask. It's tough when you're still an apprentice, going up to grown-ups who will try to make you feel stupid, then asking them questions anyway. That was good training.

Today, I get letters all the time from people who want to be columnists. They don't want to cover basic news stories, just become columnists right away. I tell them they're making a big mistake because you learn important skills as a reporter. To do anything you have to pay some kind of dues, unless you're a really great, lucky rock star. You get wonderful material, too. To see how a school board meeting works is to know why government doesn't work very well.

After being at the *Local News* about a week, I was sent to cover a speech by the chairman of the Federal Trade Commission, who was a local resident from Chester County. I went to a Holiday Inn, where the speech was given to a Rotary Club. Who really cares what the Federal Trade Commission chairman has to say? But this was Watergate for me. I was so excited. I had my notebook, my jacket and tie. I sat at the press table with other media people from the radio station and a competing paper. We all sized each other up.

His speech was probably 3,000 words. I must have taken down 10,000 words. I counted the people in the room. I was going to get all these facts. Because it was Friday afternoon for the Saturday paper and nothing else newsworthy happened, that story ended up on the front page. The headline was "Federal Trade Commission to be more active, chairman tells club." I had only used one-billionth of the facts, and the story didn't get changed much. Best of all, it had my byline. I came home with nine copies of the paper and showed everyone I knew. That's a feeling that diminishes over the years; but it's still there. When I see my name in print, it still feels good, but it'll never be as great as th.ť first time on the front page.

It was wonderful not knowing what you were going to do each day. Everyone else I knew had a routine job, but I didn't know if a plane would crash or some weird thing would happen in the newsroom, like a guy coming in with a kangaroo. You just didn't know, and that made it a lot of fun.

Since the Chester County paper was small, reporters could do whatever they wanted to. There were about ten reporters, two photographers, a sports section, a women's page. The staff was small; you knew everybody. It was a matter of what you wanted to try. I wrote a column once a week, the same kind of absolutely useless stuff I still write. That wasn't my job, but I could do it. You can't do that at *The Miami Herald.* You can say you work here, and you make more money, but you can't necessarily write a column. At the *Local News,* even though I was mainly qualified to take obituaries, I reviewed plays and covered sporting events. I even learned how to keep track of a basketball game while writing about it.

I could yell at the people in the composing room. I learned about type, about production. And I learned from my editors.

An editor, Bill Dean, had a personal history with the town and the people who lived there. I began to realize that the people I was writing about are real and what I write will affect them. He was not afraid to be critical, but he was darn careful about what he'd let you say about them. He made me aware that these were people he knew, and that the goal of journalism was not to strip them. He was a good teacher for me and taught me a lot of the nuts and bolts of journalism. For example, I didn't know how to lay out a page when I got there, but I learned page layout. One morning I was putting together the front page on deadline, and I froze up solid. I couldn't figure out where the stories should go or where the pictures should go. Bill came over and said, very calmly, "You start with this," and walked me through the page.

The managing editor was a man named Bob Shoemaker. He was good at holding back, not overreacting, not getting too excited. To a new reporter, everything's a scandal, everything's amazing, everything is happening for the first time. This is the first time a politician ever lied. Bob would always stop and reflect, and be skeptical. If there was a street disturbance, he made you look up the word "riot" in the dictionary before using it. Someone who's been around and has seen these things—not that you want to take away the enthusiasm—can help you understand the context of the news when you try to decide what approach to take.

On the other hand, you also want to keep the desire to do something new. As a columnist, I've often felt that editors tend to squelch things that are different. Innovative writing doesn't necessarily exclude accuracy. Sometimes you can take a novel approach. That's the downside to listening to the older heads. They sometimes try to force every story into formulaic writing.

As a writer, I sometimes had problems with editors. But my

real struggle as a writer came a few years later when I went to the Associated Press, where wire service writing is rigid. I lasted only about eight months. I was desperately unhappy. If I had stayed with the AP, I would have become more of an editor and less and less of a writer. After that I swore I was never going to return to newspapers and, in fact, stayed away more than seven years, teaching writing courses around the country to businesspeople. I continued to write my column for the *Daily Local News,* and although it didn't happen quickly, the column got syndicated. When I realized I could go back to newspapers on my own terms, I accepted a job with *The Miami Herald.*

I made about a billion mistakes that first year. I would do things like misspell a person's name all the way through a profile because it was a name I assumed I knew. That's very embarrassing. I once wrote a cutline that ran on the front page in which I identified a group of geese as ducks. I got 400,000 letters on that. It's amazing how easy it is to assume you know.

It was a discovery for me, too, that I was really happy doing what I'm still doing. I never thought I'd find anything. I hadn't had any goal, or sense of purpose, or long-standing ambition to work for a paper. I fell into it. And then I was so happy, I didn't care that it wouldn't pay well. Part of the reason is that I'm a skeptical person. There's also the sense that it's not brain surgery. We journalists don't take ourselves too seriously, because we're skeptical about ourselves.

I'm also a shy person in ways, and in journalism, you can be that way. It's to your advantage to hang back and watch. I remember developing the sense of being an observer. As a member of the press, you enter so many lives and institutions, impersonal situations like the school board or city counsel. You need these people, watching them and talking to them, but you're not a part of them. You'll use them and take what they give you and present it to the world. You develop a feeling of being an outsider. Your only friends are other journalists. I developed a bond with all the people who did what I did. That stuck with me. I feel as if I'm part of them. It's a bond that formed back then, that first year, that I would always want to hang around them. I like newspaper people.

Dave Barry is a staff writer for **The Miami Herald,** *where he also writes a weekly syndicated humor column. He won a Pulitzer Prize in 1988 for commentary, and his columns have been collected in three of the thirteen books he has written, which include* **Babies and Other Hazards of Sex, Dave Barry Slept Here: A Sort of History of the United States,** *and* **Dave Barry Talks Back.** *The CBS TV series,* "*Dave's World,*" *is based on two of his books. After leaving the* **Daily Local News** *he spent nearly eight years teaching writing to businesspeople. He holds a bachelor's degree in English from Haverford College.*

15

A Special License

 G E O R G E J U D S O N

My first full-time job, beginning in 1972, was not as a true re-porter. I was a rewrite man, a job I held for three years. *The Water-bury Republican* was a small paper, with a circulation of about 35,000, in Waterbury, Connecticut, and surrounding suburbs and small towns. I had taken a job there in my junior and senior years as part of the work-study program at Antioch College, to be near my high school girlfriend, and returned after graduation.

This was pre-Watergate, before journalism became fashionable, when the profession was considered slightly disreputable and the classified pages of the trade journal, *Editor and Publisher*, were filled with advertisements for newspaper reporters and editors. After Watergate, newspapers had their pick of college graduates, and there seemed to be fewer ads. Some people I worked with had been short-order cooks, one had been editing a rag in Mexico, many were alcoholic, and a few became suicides. There was this romantic scraping of the barrel that goes back to *The Front Page*. A lot of the attraction was the unconventional lifestyle. You did your work, and then you closed the bars down. Afterward, you played poker until four in the morning. It was a way to feel very worldly without any sense of responsibility. Given the times, it happened to mesh with my arrested state of development.

Once you got outside Waterbury itself, most people doing reporting were part-timers, or stringers, paid fifty cents for every inch of copy. Many were housewives. My job was to take their stories over the telephone, information that someone had gathered, in some cases willy-nilly, and I would write it as quickly as possible into a standard daily journalism story, conforming to who, what, when, where. I made sure that the "news," which was readily evident to me, ended up at the beginning of the story and was clear to the reader. Since stringers generally wrote about very localized events, such as a small-town budget argument, they often didn't know how newsy their article was. My instinct was to be on the lookout for the larger context. For example, I knew that budget problems reported from one town were happening in other towns. I put in what I knew from the other towns and changed the perspective. What would have been a brief article inside the paper would often turn out to be a page-one story because a rewrite man like me recognized that it was newsworthy.

The stringers got the byline. But one of the things that happened to me because I was doing rewrite was that I submerged my own personal investment in the stories. It didn't matter to me that someone else's name appeared over what was substantially my work, or that someone else's name appeared on a story that wouldn't have appeared on page one if it weren't for me. It was just neat that I could take a collection of sentences that sounded like the minutes of a meeting and made sense only to people who had attended the session, and make it much better by rewriting it into a genuine newspaper article that would tell readers about the town where they lived.

After a number of years I became an editor and have spent most of my career as an editor. And to do that well, you have to keep your ego half in a box. You have to be a facilitator and help other people improve their work to get the recognition that everyone wants. Others might bleed openly and publicly if they did a lot of work and didn't get explicit credit for it. But I found it was fine to be in the background.

My boss, Chuck Dixon, did this, too. His title was state editor. He was in charge of all news outside the city, and he took me under his wing. We were sitting in the office one afternoon and heard over the police radio that a two-passenger plane had crashed. We went to the crash site, which was crowded with police cars, ambulances, fire and rescue trucks. He just walked right up to where the police and others were standing. One by one, he talked to each person in charge. He wasn't demanding, but he gave off this expectation that he should know what was going on, that it was perfectly natural for him, a reporter, to be there. He asked straightforward questions about the cause of the crash and the names of the victims, but he seemed equally interested in what those guys were doing. He shared their sense that something exciting had happened. Here was someone right in front of me, approaching the police in ways that made them talk naturally. Within fifteen minutes he had learned everything the officials knew.

He was someone who had been a reporter very early, straight out of college, and had left reporting after several years to go into public relations. He'd gotten fairly high in Aetna's public relations department, but he couldn't stand it anymore. He hated the public relations life, describing it as too bureaucratic with nothing left to serendipity.

Just before I started working at the *Republican* (now the *Waterbury Republican-American*), he began working there, making half the money he had been making at the insurance company. But he was back in the newspaper business, released from the routine he'd been doing all those years, and everything was exciting to him.

The death knell to journalists is when they're bored by what they see: A police reporter goes to a murder scene, and it's just another body, rather than a body that makes the reporter wonder who that person was. But here was someone—even though he was working for a paper that was much smaller than any paper he had worked for before—who'd look around and say, "This is exciting." I fed off his enthusiasm for a number of years. To this day, he still talks about a bust of a suburban whorehouse, when he sneaked around in the bushes one night waiting for the police to arrive. It was a small, sleazy operation that a lot of people knew about and didn't much care about, but he loved being on the scene, then making what he saw into a compelling news story.

He came from the school of writing where you're supposed to write the shortest, most concise, and most interesting lead paragraph that you can. He had started at *The Arizona Republic*, where, he said, people weren't allowed to write first paragraphs longer than nineteen words. Because of him, I spent the first few years of my career writing leads and counting words, shortening them and writing them out again, and shortening again, over and over.

A favorite lead that he had prepared (just in case) was a single-word lead: "Back." Second paragraph: "That's what Jesus Christ was yesterday."

This hard-nosed approach to prose captured my fancy. Now that I'm at *The New York Times*, my leads are forty and fifty and sixty words, and editors tell me to go back and shorten them. But he made me realize that you could always make something better. It sounds kind of trite, but when you're twenty-two years old and think you're the smartest, best writer around, it was good advice.

I'd work Wednesday through Friday doing rewrite, and on

weekends, I was Chuck Dixon's assistant. Where he was in charge of news outside the city during the week, I was in charge on weekends, going out and covering what we saw as the biggest story on that day. A stringer called to report a fire at Fairfield Hills Hospital, a mental hospital located nearby. We decided that the story was big enough to send a staff person. I drove to the hospital, and in fact, it wasn't a big deal. But I spent a good part of the day wandering around the mental hospital, a place I'd never seen before, which had a room where they once applied electric shock treatments and that looked like a set for *One Flew Over the Cuckoo's Nest.* It was often like that, my ending up in a place I never had any thought of going when I woke up in the morning. I loved the lack of routine, of not knowing what someone would tell me on the telephone, of deciding myself what I would do on a particular day and then walking into work and doing something entirely different because that's what the news was.

Early on, I did a series exploring the country-and-western subculture in Connecticut, which unless you were a part of, you didn't know existed. One afternoon I went to a horse farm in a rural suburb of New Haven, owned by rodeo performers who had chipped in money to buy cattle for steer roping. As I watched these cowboys rope steers, I stood alongside the person who had introduced me to it—Malcolm Baldridge, then chairman of Scovill Manufacturing who was later to become U.S. secretary of commerce. I had first interviewed him in his office, where he kept a mechanical bull-roping device. He would sit at his desk, and while we talked, he would try to rope the hind legs of this device. The editors gave me time to work on the series, and I produced stories that ran on page one. The first one ran prominently but without my byline. Instead of being thrilled that week, I felt there was something in every paper in which these stories appeared that destroyed all my hard work.

I realized that I was developing a perfectionist syndrome that is an editor's trait. We were still using IBM electric typewriters. I'm a good typist, but if I made a mistake, even on the last line of a page, I would type it over again. It's okay to strive for perfection when you're an editor, because when you fail it's not your name on the story. When you're a reporter striving for perfection, you still have to hand your story to other people who are editors, and God knows what they'll do to your copy. One of my goals was to be a good enough writer so no one would ever touch my writing, to improve to the point where editors could not improve my copy. If they had no reason to touch it, they wouldn't screw it up. Once I started meeting that goal, I expected everyone else around me to not screw up.

I left the Waterbury newspaper after four years and swore I'd never come back to journalism. One of my complaints was that the collaborative effort of daily newspapers subjects people who are trying to do something well to too many vagaries out of their control, like the forgotten page-one byline. This, of course, was immature of me. Nearly all work requires collaboration, which means that someone almost always is left dissatisfied about something, or feeling that he or she didn't get due credit. But I had to work in a different field before I understood that. I spent a year writing what I hoped would become a novel (it didn't) and then worked in public relations for Tulane University in New Orleans. Eventually I realized I was better at journalism and returned to Connecticut and a job at *The Hartford Courant*.

Although I was fairly seasoned, having taken obituaries and having covered the town of Waterbury during college, other reporters who arrived at the paper when I did were assigned to cover specific towns and everything in it: the planning and zoning commission, the zoning board of appeals, and all the minutiae of the town. They had to have stories every day whether there was news or not. I realized during that first year that what they were learning (and that I was not learning as a rewrite man) is that they had to go back to the same people day after day and develop relationships that got beyond the superficial, to find out what was going on that wasn't quite public. They had to learn to be better reporters than I was required to be. I might have been a better writer, but they were actually learning how to be beat reporters. I've never overcome that. I'm still not a very good beat reporter in the sense of being able to peel away people's public faces and find out what's going on within their world instead of within the world they share with the public.

Whoever covered the police department had to beat their heads against the wall every day just to find information that the police should have made available but wouldn't release. The education reporter had continuing fights with the board of education, which tried to close meetings. To get access to records not made available as they should be, or to get meetings opened, he had to find people who would trust him and leak things to him. That strikes me as an essential experience that I skipped because of what was good fortune at the time—I was promoted very quickly—but it's a building block that I didn't get. This is a very basic part of reporting, to deal with that kind of resistance from the same people upon whom you are dependent for news, and to get what you need without burning bridges.

Because the Waterbury school board closed its meetings to the public, which violated Freedom of Information laws, the newspaper decided, after campaigning to gain access, to send the education reporter to a meeting with instructions to walk in and refuse to leave. When he did, he was arrested, but eventually, the board changed its policy. This was all very small-town, and even though I was learning from his experiences, I had trouble matching myself to reporters like him.

People who become confrontational reporters like confrontation. They come to journalism because they want to know everything that's going on. They are the investigative reporters, who are almost never the good writers, but who actually find out stuff that's being hidden. My friends that first year were that kind. They liked to get right in the middle and bang away as if they were participants.

Others like to hang back on the outskirts and observe and write. I was that kind of person. I fell into journalism because circumstance brought me to it. I liked to write. I liked being free to observe people. And I enjoyed trying to impose my sense of order on other people's activities or lives. Readers would learn things according to what I found interesting. When I was working on the country-and-western series, there was no hard news going on, no specific event, no action to be on the inside of. These were people living in a way that struck me as saying something about the place where we all were living, a phenomenon that played against the expected Connecticut lifestyle. To report the story, I hung out. Rather than schedule thirty-minute interviews, I spent evenings with the rodeo people or at a Hartford radio station that played country-and-western music. If you had a paper entirely made of one kind of journalist, it would either be a very superficial, shallow paper, although well written, or extremely dense and informative but unreadable. There has to be room for both kinds.

I was also involved in the newspaper union and had a number of friends at other papers who lost jobs because of strikes. My parents despised unions and my being a member was new and different for them, but it made sense to me. I was working in a city where the workforce was heavily unionized, where brass mills were shutting down every month, and where the labor beat was the premier reporter's beat. When you got your union card, you were proud to have it. I remember carrying it in my wallet for years.

During my first year, I went to a few union meetings, quickly became a member of the negotiating team, and later was the president of the local for a while. Reporters who work for small papers are not paid very much, and a great deal is expected of them. They have to write two or three or four stories a day and have to work more than the eight hours called for in the contract. But with the field of journalism changing, plenty of people were looking for jobs, and you were expected to go along to get along. People who own newspapers have a very different set of goals in mind than the people who are writing and editing the newspaper. I feel lucky to be in a job where I can wander around and observe and write, because I have no instinct for making money. I can't imagine working for a corporation where the real value is making more money than last year. But you quickly realize that that's what publishers think about.

Was I comfortable that first year in my role as a journalist? I've never been comfortable. I've never gotten over my astonishment that people return my phone calls—people who don't know me and who have no reason to talk to a reporter, much less call back when they don't know why the reporter is calling. I could not believe that during the astronauts' moonwalk in space, I was able to stop people on the street, who told me how proud they were. This still seems bizarre to me. I've been handed a very special license, to talk to strangers, and I'm continually astonished that the license works.

I'm also very suspicious of how that license is used by a number of my colleagues, and by publications wherever I've worked. When I am out as a reporter, whether as a freshmen right out of college, or even now, if people start railing against the press, my first impulse is to agree with them, especially if they've been involved in a news story. They may have something legitimate to complain about because they were misquoted, or they thought something was important that the reporter didn't, or that the reporter made a mistake. At the same time, I do firmly believe that if people approach newspapers with the proper degree of sophistication—recognizing that newspapers are merely approximations of reality, a picture of what may or may not be the truth at any given time, and at their best, what one person knew at any one time—then what newspapers do is very valuable.

I've always felt this duality in what I was doing, and I bailed out for a while because I couldn't accept it. It seemed as if I was in a totally illegitimate profession. Now, having followed the path of my former boss, Chuck Dixon, I can't imagine earning my living another way.

George Judson is a staff reporter at **The New York Times,** *where he began as a copy editor and for five years held the position of assistant metro editor for regional news. After leaving* **The Waterbury Republican** *for a two-year stint as writer and editor for the Office of University Relations at Tulane University, he returned to daily journalism and was assistant metro editor at* **The Hartford Courant** *in Connecticut before joining* **The Times.** *He graduated from Antioch College with a bachelor's degree in history.*

16

A Foot in the Door

 E L L I E   M c G R A T H

As early as my freshman year in high school in Gloucester, Massachusetts, I wanted to be a journalist. Not only did I dedicate most of my extracurricular energy to the school newspaper, I also worked during high school as a freelance reporter for the *Gloucester Daily Times*, writing stories for twenty-five cents an inch. I knew that after graduating from college I would try for a job with a national, rather than local, news publication. By the time I was finishing at Mount Holyoke College in 1974, journalists had become national heroes. Woodward and Bernstein had broken the Watergate story and exposed the corruption of the Nixon administration. I saw journalism as history-in-the-making—and a way to make a contribution to society. Many others did too, and the competition to get jobs was fierce.

One of the trustees at Mount Holyoke was Hedley Donovan, the editor-in-chief of Time Inc. As editor of the college newspaper, I was in a position to meet him at a student/trustee dinner. Although on one level I was attracted to journalism because it allows shy people to ask rude questions, I was still, in fact, rather shy. It took some guts to walk up to him. But I introduced myself and told him I wanted to work for *Time* magazine.

I was compelled to be bold—and not just because I wanted to work for the magazine. I was really worried about what might happen to me after graduation. We were at the start of a bad recession. I was concerned about whether I could get an entrée into national journalism without going to graduate school first or working for a tiny newspaper in a rural pocket of New England.

Mr. Donovan was friendly enough, but he told me that he had very little to do with hiring for *Time* magazine. "You should contact the personnel department," he advised.

Personnel departments were still making recruiting trips to colleges. A man named John Titman of Time Inc. came to our campus, and I told him what I wanted to do. Soon after, I was invited to New York to interview at Time Inc. I arrived in New York assuming that I would be interviewing for an editorial position. To my complete surprise, I went through an entire day of interviews for management-training positions. What struck me was that every single manager I talked to had a calculator on his or her desk. As a longtime victim of math anxiety, I knew that any job that required a calculator was not for me.

At the end of the day, John Titman asked if I was interested in the management-training program. I was afraid to say no, because I wanted a job. But I was also afraid to say yes, because management was not for me.

"I really want to be a writer or reporter," I told him. "And I really want to work for *Time* magazine."

It was a risk, but it was the right thing to do. A Mount Holyoke graduate who had been editor of the newspaper a few years before me had gone into *Time*'s management program and was then working in circulation. She had wanted an editorial job, but because of *Time*'s separation of "church" (editorial) and "state" (publishing), she found it impossible to change venues. I didn't want the same thing to happen to me.

John Titman told me that I didn't have enough experience to get a reporter-researcher job at *Time*. He said that I needed to have five years of reporting experience or a graduate degree in journalism. He also told me that Time-Life Books was hiring researchers. If I wanted, he would set me up with the chief of research, Bea Dobie.

It wasn't exactly what I had hoped for, and he made it clear that I was on my own from then on: no more expense-paid trips. But I was eager to meet with the chief of research and did some research on my own. I found out what subjects Time-Life Books was working on. I managed to learn that the chief of research was very involved with Irish cultural projects in New York. That was a lucky coincidence, I thought, since I was in the process of writing my senior honors thesis on art and politics in the 1916 Easter Rebellion in Ireland. I also found out that Time-Life was doing a book called *The Celts* for its Emergence of Man series.

Bea Dobie and I hit it off, despite the fact that I was quite intimidated by her. She was an elegant woman who smoked using a long ebony cigarette holder. I had never seen anyone do this, except in a Bette Davis movie. She offered me a job, and I started a month after graduation.

Coming to live in New York City was frightening after growing up in a small town and attending college in rural Massachusetts. I didn't even know that there was a West Side and an East Side. Fortunately, a number of Holyoke classmates came to New York after graduation, so we had a little network.

When I started at Time-Life Books in July, my first job was to check the accuracy of the text. The Emergence of Man was an anthropology series, so I was checking for accuracy against academic sources. My first assignment was on *The Israelites.* I would spend all day long reading the Bible. Some afternoons I'd start weeping quietly while I read, because the work was too academic, too much like being in school. I wanted to be a journalist, not a junior librarian.

It was a big adjustment to lose my campus freedom. I wasn't used to being trapped in a little cubicle from ten in the morning until six at night. But although the job wasn't much fun at first, the life in New York was. Time-Life Books had hired about twenty "kids" out of college, and a lot of us lived within ten blocks of each other on the West Side. Another researcher lived in my building, and we'd walk to work through Central Park. I learned how to play squash with a coworker who belonged to the Yale Club. We'd go to the half-price ticket booth, TKTS, on Broadway and get cheap seats for plays. When there was a snowstorm, we'd telephone each other and meet in Central Park for a snowball fight. A friend from work invited me to run the six miles around the park one weekend. I liked it so much, I began running seriously and within a year or so competed in my first marathon.

That first year was a real coming-of-age experience for me. I had to learn how one behaves in a professional environment: how to dress, what to say, how to play politics. It was especially hard to call older colleagues, particularly supervisors, by their first names. Some of the series editors and chief researchers were twenty years older than I was. My instincts were to call them Miss Bushong or Mrs. Goolrick, instead of Peggy and Martha. It felt very strange to be on a first-name basis with people old enough to be my parents. But it would have been inappropriate in that environment to address them formally.

One of the most difficult situations was dealing with a series editor and an assistant managing editor who were at war with each other. I'd bring in a piece of copy, and the series editor would make some changes. Then I'd bring it to the editor at the next level, who would change it back to the original. After a couple of weeks, I was really stressed out and went to the head researcher for help. She told me there wasn't much I could do about the problem. I should just follow procedures and be diplomatic. I learned that when caught in the middle of someone else's personality conflict, the best course is to stay as professional as possible.

Assignments got better after I finished with *The Israelites.* I got to work on *The Celts* and found it rewarding to take a subject I had studied in depth and apply what I knew. It gave me a feeling of mastery. While on the American Wilderness series, I worked with environmentalists and naturalists. For a picture essay on sea turtles, I would be on the phone every day with an expert from the University of Florida. I researched a volcano picture essay for a book called *Central American Jungles,* which led to a long-standing fascination with volcanic eruptions and earthquakes.

Eventually, I was assigned to the Boating series and had an opportunity to work primarily with photographers. Many colleagues at Time-Life Books had come there after *Life* magazine folded as a weekly, so I was able to work with some of the best picture editors in the business. For a book called *Cruising Grounds,* they let me assign the photography for a chapter on the Pacific Northwest. As the film came in, I'd go through the take and make the early selections. This visual training became very useful when I was working as an editor on smaller magazines, such as *Women's Sports and Fitness,* and had to come up with illustration concepts for stories I was assigning and editing.

One of the great things about Time-Life Books was the sense of upward mobility. Both men and women worked as researchers, and there were women editors who were good role models. Time-Life Books offered two routes to get ahead. One was through text. Researchers were periodically put on writer's trials, in which they would write captions and text blocks. If editors liked their work, they'd be promoted to writer. Writers could eventually get editor tryouts.

The other way to advance was through pictures. You could work as a picture researcher, learning how to comb through collections of photo agencies, then assign photographers, and eventually become a picture editor. At Time-Life Books, the picture editor who assigned and edited the photo shoots was as important as the editor who shaped the text.

The most important thing I learned at Time-Life Books, though, was that I wanted to be in journalism and news, not research. Reporting was not a major element of these books, in terms of investigating current events or new developments.

However, I have no regrets that I got my start at Time-Life Books. I knew I wanted to work for Time Inc., and the job was a good opening. Although I had really wanted to take the summer off after college and go to Europe, as so many of my friends were doing, I made the practical decision (partly because I had very little money) and went to work right away. I was so glad that I did, because in the fall of 1974, just a few months after I started, Time Inc. put a freeze on hiring. If I had waited, who knows what would have happened?

I look at what graduates go through today to get any kind of editorial job. Even people who are just a few years younger than I am, who did exactly what I did at Mount Holyoke—and went to Columbia University Graduate School of Journalism, to boot—still couldn't get hired as reporter-researchers at *Time* because five years later there were just no openings.

When Time-Life Books announced at the end of my second year that it would be relocating out of New York City, I immediately contacted *Time* and was offered a job as a reporter-researcher.

Although it helps to have talent, timing can make all the difference. I had been fortunate to get my foot in the door when I did.

Ellie McGrath, a senior editor at Self *magazine, spent ten years at* Time *magazine, principally as a writer covering national politics and education. She also worked as a senior editor at* Women's Sports and Fitness. *She is the author of the book* My One and Only, The Special Experience of the Only Child, *published in 1989 by William Morrow. She holds a bachelor's degree in English communications and history from Mount Holyoke College.*

17

Gotta Get the Story

 JEFF ZASLOW

I knew that landing that first job would be tough. Friends of mine had taken to wallpapering their rooms with rejection letters received from newspapers. Simply sending out clips and a résumé— which would fall, unread, into some editor's stack of other unread clips and résumés—was too passive a way to sell myself. So in 1980, at the end of my senior year, I devised a grand job-search plan to make myself less faceless. As editor of my college paper at Carnegie-Mellon University in Pittsburgh, Pennsylvania, I had access to a computer that could spit out "personalized" letters. I sent "personal" letters to the editors of the 150 largest newspapers, overselling myself as just what they needed: "Dear (name of editor): I'm loaded. Loaded with pizzazz, determination, smarts, and unlimited energy. I'm just the reporter you need. I know you probably don't have any job openings right now, but I'm coming to (name of city) to visit a friend next month. May I stop by for a few minutes to introduce myself?"

A hundred or more editors who seemed to suspect I was mainly loaded with bull sent rejection letters, but about fifteen replied with letters that said, roughly: "You're right. We have no jobs. But since you're going to be in town anyway, stop by and say hello."

I bought a three-week pass on Eastern Airlines and planned a route that included those fifteen cities. The ticket cost me $500. For three weeks, I traveled the country, hitting a different city every day. It was a great adventure. I saw the insides of more newsrooms than I've probably seen in the thirteen years since. And I got a sense of the men and women who run newspapers. Most of them didn't have jobs for me, but each meeting gave me added confidence. At the *Dallas Times Herald,* the editor recalled for me his news staff's most unforgettable day—the day John Kennedy was shot. At the *Sacramento Bee,* I crossed a union picket line to go to my interview, where the editor spoke bitterly about this strike, which had plagued his paper for months.

In San Francisco, an editor told me, "Look around the room. What do you see?"

"Reporters?" I answered, not quite knowing what he was after.

He said, "You see Jewish males. I don't need any more Jewish males." Like me, he was Jewish, but he made clear to me that editors were beginning to realize that newsrooms had to be ethnically and racially diverse. Most papers had plenty of Jewish males. I didn't get a job at the *San Francisco Examiner.*

In Atlanta, the editor asked how long I'd be in town visiting my "friend." I said all week, even though I had a plane to catch the next morning. He asked if he could hold on to my book of clips—my only book of clips—for the rest of the week to show to other editors. I let him keep it, but I was distraught. My whole schedule was messed up. I had to call ahead to other cities and rearrange appointments. After waiting a couple of days at my flophouse hotel room, without hearing from him, I called the editor at *The Atlanta Journal* and said I was leaving town early and needed my book. I didn't get a job there either.

But from that trip, I got offers from papers in Charleston, West Virginia; Syracuse, New York; Norfolk, Virginia; and from the city magazine in Pittsburgh. While deciding which one to take, *The Orlando Sentinel,* which hadn't been on my tour, flew me down for an interview. Afterward, Jim Squires, the editor, offered me a job working for at least a year or two in a bureau. The paper in Norfolk, where I had interned the previous summer, wanted me in the features section, so I told Squires, "If that's the case, I appreciate your offer, but I'll be taking the job in Norfolk."

He might have thought I was a cocky kid, but I was honest. I didn't want to cover school board meetings when I could be chasing my dream of feature writing. Squires just smiled, and within a few hours, he matched the Norfolk offer and I ended up in Orlando.

On the days my stories—and my byline—appeared, I'd wake up early and head for the newspaper box, buying six copies of the newspaper. I was one of the *Sentinel*'s best customers. I worked hard, writing three or more features a week. My supervising editors—and their supervisors—let me stretch on the job. They were open to ideas, even outside our circulation area. They'd let me go anywhere in Florida if I had a good story. I'd stay in cheap motels and eat at fast-food restaurants, so my expenses would be low and they'd figure, "Zaslow doesn't cost much when he goes out of town." Then they'd send me back out.

I wrote about a woman with amnesia who was found walking in a park in Fort Lauderdale, southeast of Orlando. There was a lot of media attention to help identify her, and the story made the television networks. Having befriended an official at the mental hospital where "Jane Doe" was being held, I was one of two reporters allowed to interview her. My article, and the photos that accompanied it, helped a friend of hers in Orlando identify her. The friend contacted the woman's family, who flew in from Chicago to bring her home. It was a great feeling, knowing that my reporting had a purpose beyond just being published. After Jane was reunited with her family, I attended a big press conference and wrote a lead detailing the media's feeding frenzy. My editor, Bill Dunn, read it and said to me, "You know what? People don't want to read that. You're going to do a lot of stories in your career. The media will always be there. That's not the story." He was right.

Sometimes readers try to define the story. I spent a "liberty" night off with a group of Navy recruits who had just finished boot camp. This was the hardest eight weeks of their lives, many of them said. After their graduation, which I attended, and after introducing me to their parents, they showed me the "lovers' lane" located at the training center and took me to several favorite bars in town. "These Navy chicks miss sex more than we do," one "booter" told me, which I faithfully reported to my readers. "I'm going to meet a girl later on tonight, and I plan to wear a motorcycle helmet and plate armor," he said. I heard from several angry readers complaining that I had glorified sexual promiscuity. I was nervous that my editors would agree that I had gone overboard. But they stood by me, pointing out that I should write with readers in mind, but not be frightened off by the most vocal complainers. The readers that a reporter hears from do not always reflect how the majority of the audience feels about a story.

I made mistakes. I wasn't as detail-oriented as I should have been. Later, I worked at *The Wall Street Journal*, where with one mistake a writer could cost investors millions of dollars in stock fluctuations. I was deathly afraid of screwing up. Not in Orlando. At least not at first. I once spelled Phil Donahue's name wrong in a story. An editor, Dana Eagles, was livid. He said that until further notice, I had to verify every spelling and put "cq" next to each name, even Smith. I know this helped me focus on the importance of getting things right. But I hated cq-ing names like Smith. I felt I was being treated like a child.

There were times when I questioned the kind of journalism I was practicing. Shortly after John Lennon died, a distraught young woman killed herself. By the time I got to her small town, I had missed the funeral, and no one in her family would talk to me. I didn't know what to do, except that I had to get the story. I walked to her gravesite and noticed a bunch of flowers. I got down on my knees and looked through the flowers for cards—and the names of people who'd sent them. It turned out to be productive, because I telephoned these people and was able to get interviews and learn more about her. But I remember thinking, "Here I am on her grave, going through flowers! This is sick."

Farrah Fawcett was appearing at the Burt Reynolds Dinner Theater southeast of Orlando, and I couldn't set up an interview, so the photographer and I parked outside the theater and staked her out. All the while, I was thinking, "I gotta get the story!" She pulled up in her car, and we ran toward her. She covered her face so a picture couldn't be taken. Rick Wells, the photographer, was running, and I was running, and Farrah was running, and part of me was thinking, "What are we doing?" The theater managers called the cops, and we got kicked off the property. And I asked myself, "Is this my job as a journalist, to chase Farrah Fawcett while she runs away, covering her face?"

Other celebrity interviews were more successful: Bob Hope, Pierre Cardin, Joan Rivers, Ann Landers. I would do a lot of research before meeting them. I'd go to the library and read current biographies and old interviews and tried to come up with questions they might not have been asked before or information that wasn't well-known. Figuring out an angle—how to approach a story—is always a great challenge.

In 1981, rock star Tom Petty returned to his hometown in Gainesville for a concert and to receive a key to the city. A big press conference was scheduled. Beforehand, I spent time in Gainesville interviewing his friends and visiting his father, who still lived in Petty's boyhood home. There on the bookshelf I found a *Boy Scout Handbook*. On the inside cover, in the script of a nine-year-old, was written "property of Tommy Petty." The rock star was once a nine-year-old scout. Instead of merely reporting what was said at the press conference, I was able to tell the story about the boy, Tommy Petty, a story that other reporters didn't have.

Ann Landers and I hit it off, and I noticed during our interview that she asked as many questions as she answered. I figured that's why she's a good advice columnist. She's interested in people. After the story ran, we corresponded and she wrote, "I know we'll meet again." Then, at *The Wall Street Journal*, while working on a story about a search to replace Landers (who was moving from the *Chicago Sun-Times* to the *Chicago Tribune*), I entered a contest seeking a new advice columnist. I only wanted the story. Instead, I got the job. Of course, I had never planned to be an advice columnist. But here I was, just as she had told me during our interview in Orlando: "Life is what happens to you when you're making other plans."

After a few months in Orlando, I was offered a job at a newspaper in Atlanta. My editor at the *Sentinel* promised me a $100-a-week raise to stay—which was a great deal of money. So I stayed. Several months passed, and the $100 never showed up in my paycheck. Finally, I got up the nerve to ask about it. I was told that employees couldn't get raises of more than 20 percent of their salaries. The editor, the executive editor, and the editor in charge of features had agreed to an $83-a-week raise, which wouldn't become effective until my next evaluation, scheduled for three months later.

The next morning I went to the head of my department with a practiced speech in hand. They had made me a promise. Before I could say anything, he told me they had agreed on the $100 raise, a result, I'm sure, of my complaint the previous day. I realized that you shouldn't be afraid to be an advocate for yourself. Reporters are valuable. Newspaper publishers can't sell newspapers without them.

The great thing about being a journalist is that you're forced to jump into the community and learn from it. I once interviewed widows and daughters of Confederate soldiers. While in their living rooms, I was very conscious of not being from the South. A northerner doesn't necessarily identify himself or herself by region; a southerner almost always does. To these women, the Civil War was not a long-ago piece of history. It was a part of their present lives.

Although papers should hire local people who have an understanding of a city's history, bringing in outsiders can offer fresh perspectives and keep a paper from becoming too provincial. I wrote a story about midgets and other small people who play the characters at Disney World. I was on a mission to unmask Mickey Mouse. Though forbidden by Disney management to speak to reporters, the characters grumbled to me about low pay and poor working conditions. They said the temperatures in their bulky, smelly costumes climbed to well over a hundred degrees. Some said they wore protective cups because youthful park visitors often kicked them between the legs. In the article, I gave away all the secrets. I was single and childless and taken by the idea of "the public's right to know."

I'm not sorry I wrote that piece. Disney is a huge employer in central Florida, and a newspaper has a right to report working conditions in its community. But now, having visited Disney World with my two toddlers and having seen the magic through their eyes, I understand better why Disney had argued with me about preserving the fantasy. Soon enough, kids grow up and realize the world is full of many truths that have been kept from them. Right now, mine needn't know that Mickey Mouse is a sweating man or woman in a costume.

That first year in Orlando, I was a twenty-two-year-old idealist who believed in the media, right or wrong. I had felt the same way when I was editor of my college paper. A student was found dead in his dorm room, and we ran a front-page story reporting that he had been dead for two days, and that his body was found because of the stench. Later, the father of the boy called me and said, "You know, I understand your need to tell this story of how he died, but you didn't have to keep repeating everything in such detail. It was hurtful to us." These days, I'd rather lose a story than get one that borders on poor taste. But it took some years to hear what that father had said.

Jeff Zaslow, the advice columnist at the Chicago Sun-Times, *writes a syndicated column, "All That Zazz." After leaving* The Orlando Sentinel, *he worked four years at* The Wall Street Journal. *While researching a story, he entered a contest seeking a replacement for Ann Landers and got the job. He holds a bachelor's degree in creative writing from Carnegie-Mellon University. He is the author of* Tell Me All About It, *published by William Morrow, and* Take It From Us, *published by Bonus Books of Chicago.*

18

Michael and Me

 L. CAROL RITCHIE

Michael Moore, who had made a national name for himself when he wrote and directed *Roger and Me*, a film about labor problems at General Motors, was looking for someone to help with his alternative newspaper, *The Michigan Voice*. He had expanded *The Flint Voice*, where he covered local stories, into a statewide paper. He had only volunteer and part-time help and needed someone full-time.

This was the spring of 1984, and I had been working in public relations at the Michigan Opera Theater, which was the only job I could get. The year before, I had graduated in the midst of a recession from Kalamazoo College with a degree in English. Detroit was a lousy area for employment. I knew I wanted to go into journalism, but I didn't know how to get a job. There was virtually no one at my small liberal arts college who had gone into newspapers who could tell me, for example, that you look for jobs at small suburban papers first. But I had had an internship at *The*

Metro Times in Detroit, the alternative weekly, and my former editor introduced me to Michael.

I had dinner with him at a pizza place right near Greek Town in Detroit. I sat across from him, facing a brick wall and listening while he set out a plan: He wanted someone to put together the whole newspaper—to write stories, sell ads, edit, help work with volunteers, and raise donations. The newspaper operated mainly on donations. Harry Chapin, the musician, and the Mott Foundation were among those who had given him money to start *The Flint Voice*. Michael is very charismatic. He's very intelligent. He knows how to sell things and make things sound good. That evening he sold me on the idea that I could do it, and that he would help me. He knew how to run a paper, he said, and I would be in charge of my areas.

The idea of working for the *Voice* was just cool. This was the hippest example of alternative culture. His politics were the same as mine, which were very liberal. The people involved were politically aware, very opinionated. They paid attention to events, were thoughtful and critical, and it seemed very exciting. I thought this would be good for me to do because I could believe in it.

A few weeks later we both agreed that we'd try it out. For a while I commuted from my parents' home in Royal Oak, a suburb of Detroit, to Flint. That was rough, and eventually I got my own apartment closer to work. The office was in an old clapboard house. Michael and I worked in the main room downstairs, which had two desks, a small reception counter, and a back door leading to a parking lot. It was the same house where Michael had worked since graduating from high school. It used to be a birth control counseling center, one of the very first in Flint. Upstairs was a little bathroom and small bedrooms. The brightest was used for typesetting and layout. Another was a scary storage room containing back issues and materials from the counseling center. I don't remember anyone ever cleaning it.

The hours were generally from nine to five, the first real hours the paper ever kept. Although I had a coffeemaker, it never worked. Michael had me organize the books. The paper had never had an ad-rate schedule. There was a poorly functioning computer with a subscription list. He had me work on subscriptions, which included writing letters to old subscribers who hadn't renewed. We took one trip to Grand Rapids and met with several peace-and-justice organizations to get more subscribers and support, and to make sure that issues of our paper were at their meetings.

At that time we were publishing monthly. I wrote inside stories and edited some articles, which I had done in college. I learned how to write just by practicing, not from any real direction or guidance. I did a lot of the layout. I had done typesetting in the past, and I knew how to work with the typesetter. Michael wrote most of the cover articles. One of his favorite covers had a picture of Walter Mondale and Ronald Reagan ripped in half. The headline was, "The evil of two lessers."

That first six months, I didn't learn much about journalism. Instead, I learned how to write about alternative issues, and I learned about writing position papers. Eventually, I got tired of knowing the outcome of a story before I had looked into it. Michael would assign stories that he knew about and give me the political slant—who the bad guys were—and it was agreed which way I would write it. I felt handicapped. I didn't know how to do in-depth reporting. I was writing only one side of a story.

Mostly I learned about politics, just from people sitting around and talking. Michael is an intellect but not an academic intellect. He hadn't gone to college. He was proud of his blue-collar roots, and his father was a longtime member of the United Auto Workers. He was always working on plant-closing issues and big General Motors issues. He introduced me to a lot of volunteers, a real mix. Some were prominent people from Ann Arbor, a counterculture haven an hour from Detroit, and some were from Flint. His volunteers absolutely adored him. He could flatter people and inspire them and make them do a lot for him. If I talked to the volunteers, they would say, "Why isn't Michael talking to me?"

I picture him sitting in that desk across from me. He is tall, but he slouches, and I never saw him wear anything dressier than a tweed jacket with corduroys. He reminded me of David Letterman, because he has a face that can scrunch up to look very kooky, and because he has such a sharp sense of humor. He could talk really well. He talked his way into persuading me to do what I probably couldn't have done, the same way he got financing for *Roger and Me*, basically with credit cards and help from his friends. I was bowled over by him. But Michael and I had our problems. I was his very first employee. He had never been an employee of anyone else. He had a hard time giving up responsibilities for sections of the paper. His lack of experience in this area had a major impact on how we worked together.

He's also a real character, a real personality, and it's hard to work for a personality. He would be late turning in stories. I'd be dependent on that material to lay out the page and would be left in the lurch. I really liked him, but I really hated working for him. I was intimidated by him and shouldn't have been. Working for strong personalities is a continual learning process for me, especially back then when I was still very young and not self-confident. But I can get a better perspective on people I work for now because of my relationship with him.

About three months into the job, I realized that our problems stemmed from the fact that he had run this publication forever, and it really was his baby. He wasn't ready to give up parts of it. I ended up trying to do his ideas, but I didn't have the confidence to say, "I have to do this on my own." A small part of me thought I could do what he was asking—putting together the whole paper—and get good writing experience in the process, especially if I could throw myself into it heart and soul. But I just couldn't get creative over circulation schemes or ad campaigns. What I really wanted to do was be a reporter, and this job was not being a reporter. It was being a jack-of-all-trades: I was a salesperson; I got papers to places; I thought about money a lot, when there was none; I handled circulation and advertising. I probably got more experience than I wanted on the pitfalls of small operations. There were all kinds of ways to lose money. Money was what this newspaper really needed, not another writer. I didn't want to think about money.

Around Christmas, Michael and I had a problem over work hours. I wanted to come in late the day after Christmas. He wouldn't let me. Disagreements must have been building up, and by then we were both fed up with each other. A week later we agreed that it would be mutually beneficial if I looked for another position. I don't know if I would have quit first or he would have fired me. I worked a couple more weeks.

But during my time there, I had talked to a lot of people and had learned about the region. I made good contacts, and that's how I ended up getting my next job—at *The Dearborn Press & Guide*, a weekly paper in Dearborn, a large suburb of Detroit. I had heard about it through one of the volunteers at the *Voice* who did free-lance photography for the Dearborn paper. Six months later I would discover that jobs at daily newspapers were scarce for people from weeklies. I would need a graduate degree in journalism in order to make the leap to a daily, where space is limited and you have to do stories in one day instead of a week. But Dearborn was a good place to start.

The editor in Dearborn was a Republican, conservative guy,

less of a personality than Michael. I was much happier there. There was coffee every day. It was stable financially, where the *Voice* wasn't; it had been in the community for years, where the *Voice* hadn't; and it was reliable if a bit dull, where the *Voice* was sometimes late and usually feisty. The editor hung out with the mayor. Michael usually opposed Flint City Hall.

I was the education writer, learning both sides of issues, making the story more complex, rather than just taking the liberal point of view. I learned about tax millage rates and school boards and elections. Because Dearborn has a large Arab population, the school system had a good bilingual program. It had been taken for granted for several years. About the time I arrived, the program was suffering a backlash among those who thought foreign students should be forced to learn English in regular classes. Bilingual advocates say students need to keep pace with their new peers by learning the subject in their own language. This was a story with good arguments on both sides of the issue.

I also wrote about Dearborn's black residents, who numbered eighty out of a population of 90,000, which is unusual because the community borders on Detroit, with a majority black population. I sought out the few black families in Dearborn and interviewed them and talked to their kids in school. Most of the families lived in a neighborhood of fairly new condominiums because the older, established neighborhoods were less welcoming. Many worked at large companies such as Ford Motor Company or Henry Ford Hospital, not the small businesses. The people I interviewed agreed that people in Dearborn were generally friendly and only needed exposure to blacks to change their fears and preconceived notions. However, residents of one white neighborhood located on the Detroit border got the city council to pass a law forbidding "out-of-towners" whom they could "see from their windows" from using their park. The ordinance was overturned in federal court. I won an award from the Michigan Press Association for the articles.

John Foren, the person covering city hall, was a role model. He sat near me, and although he didn't teach me, I could see how he covered stories, especially those that I wouldn't ordinarily read. He was good at getting news features out of boring public meetings. He was hardworking. I could hear him on the phone when he interviewed people. He was very straight with sources. People trusted him.

In Dearborn, I found I wanted to shy away from a liberal point of view, although I believe that you can't be completely objective in reporting and that you probably shouldn't be. There is a difference, however, between digging for answers to questions on both sides of an issue and clinging to a particular viewpoint. I like advocacy journalism. Mainstream papers get very boring when they try to stay so carefully and fearfully in the middle. But I tried it before I was ready, and was left with Michael's view instead of building a worldview of my own.

I later moved to Nashville, where I covered the environment, and that allowed me to write profiles, feature stories, or reports of regular meetings if I wanted. I was able to look at both sides of very tough issues. Good journalists can uncover complexities for a reader—not necessarily what the right answer is, but what the real story is. That's the journalist I want to be.

L. Carol Ritchie is a reporter with **Congressional Forecast** *in Washington, D.C. After receiving her master's degree in journalism from the University of Michigan, she worked as a reporter at the* **Detroit Free Press,** *then moved to the* **Nashville Banner** *in Nashville, Tennessee, where she covered the environment. She was named Conservation Com-*

municator *of the Year in 1993, an annual award given to print or broadcast reporters by the Tennessee Conservation League, the state affiliate of the National Wildlife Federation. She has a bachelor's degree in English from Kalamazoo College.*

19

A Good Story Stays with You

 M I C H A E L A G O V I N O

Working full-time at *Esquire* was totally different from my internship there. As an intern, I put in my fifteen hours a week doing research. I didn't know many people except the research editor, the research staff, and one of the assistant editors. I didn't know the day-to-day goings on, the egos and the politics, or even how the magazine was put together. I was given a manuscript and would check some facts, and that would be it. Then, in May 1991, five months after graduating from New York University, *Esquire* hired me as a proofreader/copy editor.

In college, I had aspired to be a sports reporter and worked briefly, very, very briefly, as a sports copy editor at the New York *Daily News.* I had connections there from my college paper at New York University. One of our former sports reporters who worked at the *Daily News* called me up one day and said, "They're looking for a part-time sports copy editor for Saturday night to edit high school sports stories. If you're interested, you should get your ass down here."

This was in September 1990, during my senior year, just after I had started my internship at *Esquire*. I went to the *News* building and met the Sunday sports editor. I was nervous, but we hit it off. "Come in Saturday, and we'll try you out," he said. "You'll get full wages." This was almost $150 for one day's work! I couldn't believe it. I was kicking my heels. My parents were overjoyed. I told the people at *Esquire*, and they said to go for it.

That Saturday night at the *Daily News*, I was very nervous. I didn't think I did such a good job, but the two men I knew there—former reporter Anthony Reiber, and our faculty adviser, John Gruber—must have sung my praises. When I later spoke to the Sunday editor, he said, "Hey, you did really well. Definitely come back next Saturday; maybe we can push it to two days a week, Friday and Saturday night."

I'm thinking, "Oh, my God, $300 a week, and I'm still in school!" That was on a Tuesday. By Thursday, there was an incident with the truckers in Brooklyn, and on Friday the *Daily News* was on strike. I didn't even go down there on Saturday. My two friends on the sports desk were big union guys. I would have been screwing them over. There was no way I was going to cross the picket lines.

I was disappointed, yes, but I had plenty to do—sixteen credits at NYU, working on the school's daily paper, and I still had the *Esquire* internship. The internship got me a full-time job here. The job just fell in my lap. I had sent out just ten résumés. My friends were sending out dozens and not getting calls back. In magazines, it's who you know, and I had the connection from the internship, having worked for two young, talented editors, Mark Warren and Chris Raymond, who recommended me. I just happened to luck out.

My duties at the beginning were kind of humdrum. I input editor's corrections into the computer. I did line reading, where I compared, word-by-word, a hand-edited manuscript with the typeset galley to make sure that nothing was missed. That was a big drag. It sounds easy enough, but occasionally you will miss something. You're zoning out because you want to do more responsible work. But I was also proofreading everything in the magazine. Even some of the editors do not read *everything* in the magazine. They don't have time. But I did, and that was a good thing.

Without realizing it, I was learning about good writing just from proofreading all those pieces. My first day of work I had to proofread a long piece by Chip Brown. It was a behind-the-scenes-in-Hollywood story about the movie *At Play in the Fields of the Lord.* I hated the story. Chip has written some great things since then, and I've come to enjoy his writing more.

After a while, I began to recognize a good story, to distinguish good from bad, and actually, there aren't that many good ones. Often a story will read like a Sunday *New York Times* feature. That's fine, but it's ordinary. A magazine like *Esquire* aspires to something better—with our tradition, we should. Many times we succeed, but many times we don't.

A good piece of writing stays with you after you've read it, like a good movie. When you read a poem by Langston Hughes or something by Don DeLillo, you just put it down, or at least I do, and say, "Man, that was something else." It does something to you. Recently, Chip Brown wrote a story for us on the murder of Alan Schindler, the gay marine who was murdered by a fellow officer in Japan. It was long—sixteen book pages—but it was absolutely brilliant. It brought to light the horrible childhoods of both the victim *and* the murderer. It was a tragic story, and he did it in beautiful prose.

A lot happens to a story before I get it to proofread. A manuscript comes into the managing editor's office. Her assistant types it into the computer and sends hard copy to the editor assigned to the piece. The editor, who is in constant contact with the writer, edits for content and big conceptual changes—rewriting certain parts, restructuring other parts. When the editors are done, they send the edited manuscript to our floor, where the copy, research, art, and production departments begin to work on it.

The first year I didn't actually copyedit many manuscripts, but the last year and a half I've been given some more responsibility. The other copy editors and I copyedit on paper and then line up our questions for the editor and researcher. On rare occasions, we call the writer ourselves, but usually the editor is the go-between. Once the questions are answered, we input the corrections into the computer—a big part of my job my first year—and give the new version to the production department.

The production department typesets it into a galley form so that it looks like an actual magazine page, and then circulates it as a first galley. A couple of copy editors read it; then the research department sends more information or we get more changes from the writer and editor. One of us inputs the new changes, and production circulates a second galley. The process is repeated two more times, until our department gets "final pages." A copy editor gives it a final proofing, then inputs those corrections and signs off, hoping the piece has no mistakes. The final version is sent to production, which ships it to the printer.

During the first two weeks of the magazine cycle my hours are generally from ten to six or ten to seven. The last two weeks when we're closing the magazine—editing final proofs and shipping pages—I often work until ten at night. We hardly ever work on Saturdays, but when we do we're usually not paid overtime.

People laugh at the craft of copyediting. It doesn't command that much respect. They say, "Oh, God, that sounds boring." But it isn't boring; it's important. At least, those of us in the department think it is. Punctuation, style, consistency—we have to keep our eyes wide open. I don't have any copyediting pet peeves, but sometimes I do get mad at writers. They often have such a high opinion of themselves, and most of them aren't as good as they think. We can't touch the copy of certain writers because they're so prominent, and that annoys me.

I *did*, however, get to copyedit a manuscript that Norman Mailer wrote for our Sixtieth Anniversary issue. Mailer loves boxing, and he wrote an essay on his personal boxing experience. Naturally, he was given a lot of leeway. There were some commas, for instance, that normally would have been taken out, but since it was Mailer, the editors said, "It's Mailer, he's a legend," and we left the commas in. I know a little about boxing, too, and Will Blythe, our literary editor, surprised me by accepting a lot of my changes—more than I had expected. A lot he disagreed with, saying "No, I don't like that change." But so far, that's been the highlight of my career—that I even touched Norman Mailer's copy!

Now, Will, for instance, is a great editor to work with. Besides being an exceptionally talented writer and editor, he is nurturing; he'll sit down and listen to your questions and your ideas. A lot of editors—and magazine people in general—are self-important and arrogant; they can be difficult to work with. In magazines, maybe more so in literary magazines, there are a lot of highfalutin literary types. It's frustrating to deal with different egos, especially when two editors have different ideas about how a piece should read and I have a copyediting deadline to meet. I just have to take a deep breath, not lose my cool, and try to be as rational as possible while they're grappling with it.

It's a really strange business, magazines. Everyone is afraid they'll lose their jobs. Editors desperately have to come up with new ideas all the time, and anyone else with an idea seems to be perceived as a threat. It's particularly frustrating for the younger people, who are all very bright and could contribute more than they actually do. After a while, researchers, copy editors, editorial assistants all ask themselves, "How long do I want to do this?" I often ask myself, "How long do I want to copyedit?" I'd like more freedom to offer ideas, and I'd like to get a chance to edit stories. I'd like to write, even just two- or three-hundred-word blurbs. But you have to bide your time. Cornering the senior editor in the elevator and telling him you have all these great ideas doesn't work here. I've had better luck writing short freelance articles for *The New York Times* Style section, *New York* magazine, and *Spin*.

You can't come on strong; you can't be threatening. You have to be humble and hope that people learn to respect your intelligence. When I was at NYU, I had a journalism professor named John Katz, who writes for *Rolling Stone*. In his class, I was always the quiet one. There were a lot of precocious, confident kids in the class, and I just figured they were better than I was. But when I told Professor Katz I might major in history, he said, "No, no, you should major in journalism because you're really good. You're one of the best in the class. You write good tight leads. You write clearly and concisely." I thought he was patronizing me.

"But what about all these other kids?" I asked.

"You haven't seen their work," he said, and his encouragement led me toward print media.

At the beginning it was very exciting. I was just happy to be here. I was twenty-three, working at one of the biggest magazines in the country, and didn't mind doing a lot of the grunt work. Hey, you're a rookie; you have to do grunt work. At least I didn't type in stories. But the novelty started wearing off and I was getting impatient. It took almost three years before I was promoted to assistant copy editor.

The real behind-the-scenes life of magazines is not all that great. People think it's more glamorous than it is. When you're working long hours, not getting paid overtime, and not getting much recognition, you start to wonder if it's worth it.

I ask myself all the time whether I'd be willing to go to a less prestigious magazine, where I could do more. But if I had to do it all over again, I'd probably do the same thing. How could I refuse a job at *Esquire* magazine?

Michael Agovino is an assistant copy editor at Esquire *magazine. He is a graduate of New York University with a degree in journalism.*

20

From Fiction to Fact

 MELINDA LEWIS-MATRAVERS

I had been in Santa Barbara, California, for only seven months when a printmaker for whom I was working decided to move his studio to New York. I needed to find a new job, so in December 1987, I answered a classified ad for a receptionist at *Islands.* Though I had heard of the magazine, I had never seen it. But "islands" have always enchanted me: the island on the horizon of my Lake Michigan home; the Apostle Islands where my husband and I spent our honeymoon; and the islands that appear in the short stories I write.

I had always worked in the arts, producing performance art and dance series and fund-raising events in Washington, D.C., and Manhattan, acting as curator for the printmaker, and had recently received an M.F.A. in creative writing, but there was no work available with an arts organization or on a college faculty in town. So right before Christmas, I became a receptionist at *Islands,* answering phones, typing letters for the advertising staff, sending out the mail, and so on. I had no idea that my first weeks on the job would coincide with the beginning of the most tumultuous year in the magazine's history. The editor (now the position is called editor-in-chief), who had been with the magazine three years, left. It was not until after the New Year that a new editor was hired, and then the managing editor was fired. Four weeks later, the new editor left. That left an editorial staff of four: a production manager, a managing editor from a temp agency, an art director, and her part-time paste-up assistant.

In addition to my administrative tasks, I was occasionally asked to proofread and type manuscripts, and even to fact-check a story, including one on New Zealand. To amuse myself, and because it needed to be done, I also took the initiative to compile the first index of the magazine—seven years' worth of photocopied tables of contents stapled together had served as the previous "index."

By February—thanks to both the temporary managing editor, who moved up to editor, and the art director—a new position was created for me. As assistant editor, I now did photo research and fact checking, and also read manuscripts.

One of the first stories I was asked to photo-research was about New York's Coney Island. At that time we didn't make very many photo assignments and instead used stock images from freelance photographers and a handful of agencies. *Islands* is a glossy magazine, very dependent on images. The magazine is known for its four-color photo spreads, but to me Coney Island was a black-and-white story. Somewhere, sometime, in some gallery I had seen art photographs of the boardwalk. I began my search for those vaguely remembered images by calling the nearest photography museum, which was in Riverside, California. It had an exquisite collection of turn-of-the-century Coney Island photos printed from glass negatives, but our art director wanted more contemporary pictures. My husband is a photographer; he suggested the work of Bruce Davidson and Elliott Erwitt.

I next called the International Center for Photography in New York City, where the young man in the library then referred me to the Magnum photo agency. Magnum sent a whole stack of original 1950s Coney Island images by Davidson and Erwitt, as well as others by Eve Arnold, Henri Cartier-Bresson, and 1980s work by Ferdinando Scianna. These *were* the images I was looking for, and they were marvelous: evocative of that gritty, urban amusement scene with young lovers on the beach, a chaos of neon and Ferris wheels, the dated tawdriness of it all. They were the perfect illustrations for the story and inspired the art director to design a piece that I consider one of the best we've ever done.

As a small magazine, *Islands* didn't have a big budget for photographs. But photographers and even agencies would agree to lower-than-usual page rates because they appreciated its production values. We spend an incredible amount of money in color separation, on paper, and printing. In addition to production costs, we take on a huge liability. We use originals. We do not use duplicate photos. All photographers insure their slides. At any time, we have thousands of dollars' worth of slides in our office.

The most eye-opening thing for me that first year was being introduced to fact checking and realizing what an essential part of the magazine it is. I inherited the job from the production manager, whose main task was inputting manuscripts and coordinating the back-and-forth between the off-site typesetter and the in-house editors. Her fact checking basically consisted of verifying place-names with a seven-year-old *National Geographic Atlas* and looking up other checkable details in sundry brochures or guidebooks a writer might provide. Our research tools also included the one-volume *New Columbia Encyclopedia* circa 1975, a *Webster's Collegiate Dictionary*, a geographic dictionary, and the 1988 *World Almanac*.

When I first started, I didn't have a clue about fact checking, and neither did she. She had taken on this task when the managing editor was fired. I simply followed her tack of relying on the writers. If I encountered problems, I called, asking, "Is such and such true?" and accepted their answers. I really shudder to think about that now, because if a writer is incorrect, he or she usually is not aware of it! Interestingly, it was those photographs of Coney Island that underscored the necessity of fact checking. We received two letters from readers who were convinced the Eve Arnold photo we had used was of Atlantic City's boardwalk, not Coney Island's. This triggered a fascinating search for the "truth." First I questioned the photo agency, but Magnum stood by its identification, though it acknowledged that the photographer had also shot Atlantic City. I then consulted a couple of Coney Island historians and tracked down one in Atlantic City. Historical societies can be found in many communities, and they are wonderful sources of arcane and folksy knowledge. The local staff, often volunteers, have an enthusiastic interest in your questions and are earnest assistants. I was directed to oral histories, period phone directories, and old snapshots in an attempt to answer the Coney Island question, "Where is this?"

The photo had been taken at night. It showed the entrance to an amusement park and a neon sign of an Aunt Jemima–type figure, an inconclusive detail. Photos may not lie, but they don't speak either! In the end we printed the letters in a later issue with an editor's note that was equivocal: We left it up to the readers' judgment.

By September of that first year I was working with yet another new editor; she made the greatest impact on my career, especially on fact checking. Joan Tapper came from the National Geographic Society, where the staff is painstakingly careful. She taught me that fact checking is done to support the writer's story, but that it is also my responsibility to examine the articles critically and to be alert to what constitutes a fact. I could not shrink from checking something even if it required transcontinental telephone calls or days of research in the university library. Our own reference library expanded (the publisher brought in his family's set of *Britannica*), my Rolodex of "experts" and sources grew, and my skills at verifying quotes (a delicate matter) were perfected. (Sometimes I'd read the quote directly. More often than not, I'd verify the sense of it. When you read a quote directly, people often want to change it, because they think it doesn't sound good.) And whereas I once used only one file folder for an issue's worth of fact checking, I began to fill a file folder for each story.

I remember a story about some Irish islands that was very descriptive and seemed to really catch the spirit of the place. But when I called the author asking for his support materials to use for fact checking, he was unhelpful: In fact, he was indignant that I would even question his authority. I had to spend considerable time tracking down my own sources to support his article. After I had checked all the geographical and historical statements (including reading biographies on Irish dramatist John Synge and poet William Butler Yeats to verify—and, as it turned out, to correct—some of the author's statements), and had confirmed the spellings of Irish words, and had consulted the tourist board about other details, I still needed to call two sisters who owned a small inn and who figured quite prominently in the piece. In the course of my telephone conversation with them, I discovered that the writer's "telling" detail about an electric clock that was "mis-set" was, in fact, a battery-operated timepiece, and it kept very accurate time, thank you very much! The sisters' correction foiled the writer's symbolic detail, which represented, for him, how the islands were a place out of time. We made the change, but did the fact tell a truer story? Well, maybe not truer, but it didn't tell the truth falsely.

Writers share with politicians the tendency to believe that if they say "it" or write "it" down, then "it" must be true. But we all need to check ourselves, even fiction writers. You can't write a story about Hawaii and set it in the South Pacific. You simply can't take real places and put them in the wrong hemisphere, unless, of course, your plot concerns a dramatic shifting of the earth's tectonic plates. Otherwise, readers will, *and should*, mistrust you.

While researching the Irish islands story, I came across information about an early-twentieth-century filmmaker mentioned by the writer. This man's work and his connections with a number of islands fascinated me, and that interest became the basis for my first byline in the magazine. I wrote a sidebar about him to accompany the Irish islands story. (A year or so later I wrote a brief piece about the release of one of his films on video.)

My knowledge of geography was greatly enhanced that first year, since we do stories from around the globe. People always ask us, "Aren't you going to run out of islands?" But there are almost 14,000 in Indonesia alone, and such variety everywhere—from Muslim-influenced Lamu off the coast of Kenya, to Manhattan, to the quintessential South Pacific island of Bora Bora. Besides learning where these places were, I got a sense of what they were, what the landscape was like, and who lives there.

That first year, in addition to photo research and fact checking, I read manuscripts as they went through the editing, galley, and page-proof stages. One of my first "contributions" to a story was to put parentheses around its parenthetical phrases. I can still hear the publisher admonishing the poor unsuspecting editor about how magazines do not use parens. Magazine style, he advised him, was to use short sentences or en dashes when necessary. I never confessed to the publisher that it was I who had done such an unprofessional thing, but I did admit it to the editor. Shortly thereafter each of the three editors had a different-colored pencil to use when marking manuscripts. I still remember the color codes, and to this day I hate red-leaded pencils, mine!

That first year, I was such a novice in the field of magazines, I didn't know how the editing process worked. I didn't realize that a submitted piece could be considerably changed by editors. Suddenly the beginning was at the end, and a piece written in the third person became a first-person account.

I have learned a tremendous amount from other editors, all of whom have considerable experience: Joan Tapper was the founding editor of *National Geographic Traveler*; Dewey Schurman came from the local newspaper; Tony Gibbs from *The New Yorker* and *Yachting*. Their different editing and writing styles have been quite instructive. I particularly like the way Joan edits. She is very deft at preserving the writer's voice even when she substantially trims and reshapes a piece. Dewey edits with a newspaperman's quickness and concision. Tony edits lightly, perhaps because his own writing, which is wonderful, requires little tuning. It's fascinating how we each read manuscripts differently. My comments come from being both a fact checker and a fiction writer: I look closely and critically at details and information. If a manuscript depends on gratuitous description, empty adjectives, or offhand remarks, I become suspicious and dismiss it. On the other hand, if the piece has structural integrity, if it works as a whole, I will accept it where other editors see it as not being appropriate in style or content for the magazine.

Over the seven years I have been here, the staff has doubled, though it is still small. About twenty-five people produce the bimonthly magazine, a monthly newsletter, and auxiliary items.

Publishing a magazine is a collaborative effort, not only between editors and writers, designers and photographers, but among advertising and circulation and editorial departments (not to mention the important support work done by those on the administrative side: answering phones, making travel arrangements for the writers and photographers, and collecting money from delinquent advertisers). Working at a magazine with a tiny staff, I have been able to see the entire process in action.

My duties have expanded as well. As associate editor, I have been increasingly drawn into the review of proposals, and the search for new writers, topics, and islands. Most significant, however, is that I have been able to do some travel writing, which combines two of my favorite occupations. I shall always be grateful to the publisher who hired an overqualified receptionist and willingly moved her up the masthead.

Melinda Lewis-Matravers is associate editor of Islands *magazine. She has a bachelor's degree in English from Earlham College and holds a master of fine arts degree in creative writing from the University of Michigan.*

21

Life *in the Big* Time

 F R A N C E S G L E N N O N

I got into journalism by the back door. When I applied to personnel at Time Inc. in 1949, I was told there weren't many opportunities in editorial for a person with my background (I'd majored in economics at the University of Michigan), but there was an opening in ad promotion at *Life* magazine, which at that time published weekly. I grabbed it and stayed until 1954. It turned out to be a glamorous job—I traveled all over the country, called on department stores and menswear stores, put on retail promotions, attended conventions, and made calls with advertising space salesmen. But I kept asking myself, "What am I doing here?" I wanted to be in editorial.

I finally had a break. The magazine had engaged Gjon Mili to photograph department-store scenes—salespeople, display windows, customers—that were used for promotions targeted at salesclerks. Traveling with Gjon, I learned more about photojournalism and the people at *Life* and could observe firsthand the psyche of an artist. Gjon volunteered to help me make the move to editorial. Because he was one of the first photographers to work for *Life* and also one of the finest, his recommendation went a long way—and I soon found myself as a new researcher on the magazine.

At my going-away party from *Life* ad promotion, my colleagues presented me with a folding board of two four-foot-high photos. The picture to the left was of a vivacious young woman engaged in conversation with an advertising executive at a party; its caption: "Farewell!" That woman was me. The other showed the back of an unidentified woman in working clothes and flat-heeled shoes, head low, going out of the door of the magazine office in the dark of night; its caption read: "Hail!" It seemed all too prescient, leaving a life of glamour for the late hours and hard work in the magazine's editorial section.

I started out in the department called "World's Week," which featured noteworthy events of that week in pictures. There were only two of us assigned to it: Don Wilson, the editor, and I, the researcher. During the week Don and I went over the AP, UP, and other wire service photos that came in, and by Wednesday afternoon we had a pretty good line on what might comprise some of the pages. But we knew that we had to be prepared for fast-breaking news stories or more compelling photos that might land in our offices. Picture quality, while always important at *Life*, wasn't the major criterion in this department. We were trying to compose a montage of the week's major news events that weren't being covered elsewhere in the magazine.

By Friday morning we had collected about seventy-five photos we wanted to present to the managing editor, the legendary Ed Thompson. And this is where I got my real training in photojournalism. Ed didn't put on any pretenses; he'd casually riffle through the photos and put some aside. He was a great mumbler, aided and abetted by the cigar he always had hanging out of his mouth. We learned to see what he did, not try to hear what he said.

By the time Ed reached the bottom of the pile, he would have sifted the pictures to about seven or eight he wanted to feature in World's Week. Standing there beside him, I gradually absorbed the reasons that one photo might be chosen over another. If it was related to the same event, why this one and not that? Sometimes it was easy: A certain compelling quality was evident in the captured scene or a person's expression. In other cases, he might choose the less dramatic because he wanted to vary the pace of the section. That might mean he'd go for the picture of a fire that showed one fireman and a kid watching from across the street rather than the burning building inside. Or he'd add an amusing picture of a less consequential event (bathers at Coney Island, a bike marathon) to spice up the page. Then he'd stand back and see what he had as a whole. Through that process, I learned a good deal about photojournalism.

Pictures were the most important—but not the only part—of the operation. We also had to be prepared to write good, pithy captions. Part of our indoctrination at *Life* was the notion that a picture was indeed worth a thousand words. That meant there was a lot riding on the caption. It should be as concrete as possible, deal with what was shown in the photo—and still provide some context. All this had to be done in two or three lines of forty or fifty characters per line. Quite an exercise.

With World's Week, everything we needed in research might be found on the back of the photo. But in the limited time we had, we'd also have to cover the wire services, newspapers, and other sources such as reports from our correspondents. The pressure was on from Friday until Saturday night when the magazine closed. My job was to get the caption information together, turn it over to Don Wilson for writing, check what he had written, see it through Ed Thompson and Joe Kastner, the copy editor—then stick around until the magazine closed. If we had time to cover late-breaking news, there might be last-minute substitute pictures, and I'd have to scramble to provide salient information.

A valuable lesson in the professionalism of our trade was made vivid one New Year's Eve, which coincided with the closing date of that week's magazine. The newspeople had to be there, and some bottled cheer was brought into the office. Midway in the evening we discovered that one of our big photos in the World's Week section—of the Great Wall in China—had been taken two years earlier. (You might ask why it would matter since that wall had been around for some 2,400 years; I can only say that at *Life* it did.) Ed Thompson seemed to be the only editor around, so he was called into action. No substitute for that photo could be found at that late hour, so Ed sat down at the typewriter and deftly composed a new caption while I stood behind him for moral support. In that celebratory state, Ed was still the editor par excellence—of grace, albeit rough-hewn, under pressure.

On closing nights, it wasn't unusual for the editorial staff to stay at the office until two in the morning, and sometimes even later, until four or five in the morning. This meant that our lives revolved more and more around our job and the people associated with it. I began to spend time with people who had my own schedule. It was like being an intern in a hospital, and like interns, we began to see our work as a calling, something to which we dedicated ourselves. But we weren't likely to admit it; as journalists we knew the value of personal privacy, and our idealism was mixed with skepticism.

During that first year, I moved on to the "Picture of the Week" department, again a department of two people, but instead of eight to ten pictures, we dealt with one. It had to be exceptional enough to run across two pages, what was called a "double truck."

Newsworthiness wasn't an important criterion, but we weren't supposed to be arty either. Sometimes a particularly dramatic picture came in over the transom; in other cases we would assign pictures to be shot. When these were in the New York area, I would often accompany the photographer. On one occasion the photographer, Ralph Morse, and I were assigned to photograph three splendid white stallions as they made the jump at a Madison Square Garden horse show. We were to shoot the scene from above. (This was an idea of another photographer, Howard Sochurek, who was otherwise engaged at the time.) Ralph and I went up to the rafters at the Garden and walked around until we got the best site for what turned out to be a wonderful picture. Imagine getting away with anything like that today! For me it was what *Life* was all about then—and I, the daring young reporter.

Those of us on the staff had a lot of respect for the photographers who worked for the magazine. People like Eugene Smith, David Douglas Duncan, Gordon Parks, Margaret Bourke-White were legendary to us, and their exploits were well-known. Even before I moved to the editorial department, I remember seeing Eugene Smith in the halls when he was showing the editors his "Spanish Village" story. When we went out on assignments with the greats, and even lesser greats, we catered to them. First, get the pictures—then the words. Some of the *Life* photographers I worked with, in addition to Gjon Mili, included Alfred Eisenstaedt, Fritz Goro, Howard Sochurek, and Nina Leen. Strictly professional and unflappable, they ran the gamut—but it was a team operation, and we made it work.

That first year led to my working in the "Close-up" department, which had stories focusing on an individual. The editor, Dave Sherman, was a former photographer who went over to the text side but whose bias was still toward pictures. He and I would suggest interesting potential Close-ups, and once we had the managing editor's approval, assignments were made. I did most of the reporting on the East Coast, and this could be stimulating work. Some of the Close-ups I was responsible for were on Margaret Mead, Thomas J. Watson, James Thurber, test pilot Scott Crossfield, and Jean Kerr. As the reporter, I would accompany the photographer while she or he got the pictures, would pick up quotes along the way, and do some casual interviewing while the subject was going about his business. Then, I'd usually arrange for an interview to ask more probing questions. The result was often a mountain of material, which an editor back in New York, Dave Sherman or another, would put into correct form for the magazine. This could include a column or two of quotes that I'd provide on a variety of topics, or the quotes might all be absorbed in the story. We were a team operation, and the excitement was being out on assignment, getting to know the subject, and shaping the story with the photographer. Group journalism meant "we," not "I," and I was quite comfortable with that idea.

In the early 1950s, most women worked as researchers at *Life* (though we were all called reporters, for many it was an inside job). These women were often highly educated, extremely talented, and professional. Their attitude toward the editor, usually a male, could be quite adversarial, especially when checking the story. This adversarial attitude was much more pronounced at *Time* magazine than at *Life*, but it was one of the hazards of the trade. Our wonderful research director, Marian MacPhail, kept a sense of proportion about these matters, smoothed much troubled water—and she always backed us when we needed it. Still, most of the editors were male. You'd find women editors in so-called women's areas—fashion, home furnishings, food—but I can't remember any other departments where women held sway. Even though Time-Life was considered an enlightened company in those days, more men than women were promoted. A man might come in as a reporter, but he wouldn't stay long at that; he would soon be trained as a writer and moved up the ladder to correspondent or editor if he had promise.

Following my own natural bent, I gravitated toward more general, world-oriented departments and steered wide of the strictly women's-interest areas. I had gotten into journalism in the first place because of that kind of interest in my home. My father read *The New York Times* and my mother, the *New York Herald Tribune*, and we had lively, rather well-informed discussions at the dinner table about national and international events. Journalism was newspapers, magazines, and some radio news broadcasts and commentators. *Time* magazine was ubiquitous in our home and, yes, *Life* too.

In its heyday, *Life* had a circulation of seven and a half million, with about five hundred people on its editorial staff. Our editorial crew in New York was relatively small; about two hundred were on the masthead. It was a democratic operation with give-and-take. We were trained in group journalism, and the editors trusted us; if anything went wrong, they'd back us up. We all had a lot of pride in our product (though we'd never have referred to the magazine as a "product"). And we had esprit, which we almost took for granted. But those who had worked elsewhere knew that it wasn't the same in other places.

In December 1972 the magazine folded as a weekly, and *Life* as we had known it dissolved. It was traumatic for all of us who had spent our lives there. *Life* had been big, bold, and brash. It had what is still called *impact*. People paid attention to what was on the cover of the magazine—and to the features inside. Like the country itself, *Life* was democratic, diverse, chaotic, somewhat idealistic—and like no other place. For me—for all of us—it was the Big Time. All those years in editorial, beginning with the very first, I never again had that nagging feeling of "What am I doing here?"

Frances Glennon is an associate editor at Smithsonian *magazine, where she has been since 1982. She stayed at* Life *until 1972, spending most of the 1960s working on the editorial page. When the magazine folded as a weekly, she continued to work on special issues before moving to Washington, D.C. Glennon has a master's degree in general studies from Yale University and a bachelor's degree in economics from the University of Michigan, where she was also a Michigan Journalism Fellow.*

22

The Last Page

 MITCH GERBER

I had come back from a year of hitchhiking and working overseas and found myself that summer of 1974, at age twenty-five, back at my parents' house in suburban Buffalo with a bachelor's degree in history and no particular plans. I knew I wanted to be in journalism—my father's stories from his youth as a copyboy and cub reporter at Buffalo's morning paper had filled me with the romance of it, and I had been a summer reporter at the same daily newspaper. But life at home seemed boring after the excitement of travel. I had picked apples on a kibbutz in Israel, bounced along the Mediterranean coast in the back of a pickup truck with a crew of Turkish construction workers, and shared bread and cheese with a Croatian family in the cheap seats of a train through Yugoslavia. Now I was just hanging out with old friends and trying to reconstruct a travel journal that I had lost.

By late August I was broke enough to send out some résumés, but to no avail.

Then I saw my dentist for a checkup. I've always been good about that.

He was a long-distance runner, and while poking around my mouth he told me that another patient had just asked him to write a magazine piece about what it's like to run a marathon.

"Magazine?" I mumbled through the suction tubing.

"It's a new one," he said. "A sports magazine, called *Buffalo Fan.*"

I rinsed. This was interesting. I've always loved sports. I liked being in Buffalo. I liked the prospect of a byline even more. "Who's the editor?" I asked, trying to sound casual.

"Dick Hirsch," the dentist said. This was even more interesting. I knew who Dick Hirsch was. His father and my father were old friends. Hirsch, who was vice president of a big printing company in town, had once been a newspaper reporter. The president of the printing company, according to the dentist, had started the magazine, made his son the publisher and Dick Hirsch the editor.

As soon as I was free from the dentist I called Hirsch. "Need any help with the magazine?" I asked.

"Come in at eight-thirty tomorrow morning, and we'll talk," he said.

I am not a morning person, but the next day I showed up at the printing plant and gratefully accepted an offer of coffee. I was thinking, "Just let me finish this cup, please." But Hirsch called me into his office. We talked for a while, and then he pulled out a manuscript and said, "Tell me what you'd do with this." It was a feature piece about the Buffalo Sabres hockey team, written by a local sportswriter.

The story opened with the writer speaking in the first person about how he set out to gather the information. The second paragraph was about the appeal of the Sabres' leading scorer, who was both a great sports hero and a terrific personality. He had real star quality.

I crossed out the first paragraph.

I went through the first couple of pages. I forgot the time. I forgot the coffee. While Hirsch was busy with printing-company business, I was discovering that I loved making another writer look better. I'd never taken an editing course, never done any professional editing. I had graduated from Columbia University and had had one summer's experience as a copyboy and two summers as a reporter, plus the usual school-paper reporting. This was new to me. But I just knew what needed to be done to that copy.

Then Hirsch interrupted. "Let's see what you've got," he said.

He looked it over. He went to consult with the president of the company. I drained my cold coffee and waited. Hirsch came back. "How would you like to be assistant editor?" he said.

I was amazed. I was expecting a freelance writing assignment at best, not a job offer. I forgot to ask how much, or to tell him I'd have to think about it. "Uh, sure," I said. I held that job for three years, and I've been in magazines or newspapers ever since.

As the assistant editor, I line-edited just about everything that went into the magazine. Hirsch set policy and made story assignments and usually talked to the writers, but his main job was being a successful printing salesman, and the company didn't want him taking too much time away from that. Once the stories were in hand, it was my responsibility to whip them into shape.

I wrote most of the headlines and also wrote two or three stories for each issue, under different bylines. One of them was Miriam Blake, the restaurant reviewer. Since the magazine couldn't afford to send me to all the restaurants I had to review (except for the time we rated local pizzas), I would get a copy of the menu and weave an imaginary meal from it. As far as readers knew, the restaurants were all superb. But I understood even then that these were dues I had to pay. Hey, I was glad to be working.

That year I learned a lot about where a good lead might be hidden. Hirsch had assigned a story to a sportswriter in Jamestown, New York, a small town southeast of Buffalo with an incredibly successful community-college basketball team. The team would go 22–3, 21–5 year after year and played in national tournaments. The young coach would travel to inner cities around Jamestown—like Buffalo, Pittsburgh, and Cleveland—find these great players and convince them they could be stars at his school. Some of them were. But because most were black and poor, they didn't really fit in with the demographics of Jamestown, which was virtually all white, or the lifestyle, which was remote from anything these guys had known.

None of that was in the manuscript that came in. It was pretty much a puff piece, full of praise for the coach and the school. Hirsch had me read it. "There's nothing here," I reported back.

"Let me see it," he said. On what must have been the last page of a twenty-page story, he pointed to a line and said, "Look at this." It was the briefest mention of the players' social lives, about how they had to find apartments together in town—there were no dormitories—and spent all their time together outside class.

"That's the story," Hirsch said. He was right.

The writer, who lived in Jamestown and had an ongoing relationship with the college, reluctantly rewrote the piece. In the course of editing and asking more questions, we learned that at least two players had quit school and gone home, feeling miserable. And even though the writer didn't have his heart in it, we edited the article carefully, and it turned into a terrific piece that readers, sportswriters, and reporters at other papers talked about. It was the kind of story you always remember.

Most of all, it taught me that, one, leads are not necessarily up front, and two, don't give up on a story until you get to the last page. It's a lesson that has paid off for me more than once. That first job led to my next one, and that one to the next. Wherever I've been, though, I always go to the dentist. You never know.

Mitch Gerber, who edited Sunday magazines for newspapers in Buffalo, New York, and Orlando, Florida, and who was a copy editor at Newsday *on Long Island, is managing editor at* Washingtonian *magazine, in Washington, D.C. He has a bachelor's degree in American history from Columbia University.*

Index

Accuracy, 49–50, 64
  checking for, 133–34
Advice columnists, 143
Advocacy journalism, 152
African-American journalists, 51–52
African-Americans, 151–52, 180
Agovino, Michael, xvi, 154–60
Air and Water News, 81, 82–86
Allen, Frank B., 75–76, 77–78
Alternative culture, 147, 148, 149
Angle, Martha, 58
Arnold, Eve, 163, 164
Associated Press (AP), 73, 119, 170
Atlantic Monthly, 87

Barrett, Betty, 88–89, 93, 94
Barry, Dave, xv, 115–20
Bernstein, Carl, 63, 131
Black Alumni Network, The (newsletter), 51–52
Black Journalists, The NABJ Story (Dawkins), 51
Blumenstyk, Goldie, xvi, 27–35
Blythe, Will, 158
Bourke-White, Margaret, 173
Brown, Chip, 156
Buffalo Fan, 178–81
Bureau reporter(s), 30–35
Burgard, Steve, 50–51
Burgin, Dave, 36–37, 40–41
Burritt, Burton, 74–75, 77
Business journalism, 92, 94
Byline, 5, 23, 117, 122, 140, 166, 178, 179

Camaraderie, 17, 60–61, 66
Campbell, Mary Ann, 31–32
Captions, 171–72
Careful Writer, The (Bernstein), 40
Carter, Betsy, xv, 81–87
Cartier-Bresson, Henri, 163

Case, Ted, 111–12
Ceppos, Jerry, 107
Chapin, Harry, 147
Charnley, Mitchell V., 74–75
City editor(s), 23
Civil rights movement, 53, 57, 60
Clarity, emphasis on, 70
College journalism experience, 20, 28, 51, 53,
    54, 63, 73, 105, 126, 138, 145, 154
Columnist(s), 118
  advice, 143
  syndicated, 119
Cooney, Beth, xvi, 1–8
Copy editor(s), 157–60
Copyboy, 21, 179
Cub reporter(s), 21, 22, 106

Daily Argus, The, 44–51
Daily Local News (West Chester, Pa.), 115–19
Dan's Papers, 18
Davidson, Bruce, 162, 163
Dawkins, Wayne, xvii, 44–52
Deadlines, 11, 56
Dean, Bill, 118
Dearborn Press & Guide, The, 150–52
Democrat and Chronicle (Rochester, N.Y.),
    105–14
Des Moines Register, The, 75
Details, 41, 49, 50, 68, 69, 70, 167
Disney World, 144–45
Dixon, Chuck, 123–24, 125, 130
Dobie, Bea, 133
Donovan, Hedley, 131–32
Duncan, David Douglas, 173
Dunn, Bill, 141

Eagles, Dana, 141–42
Editing
  magazine, 167

Editor and Publisher, 121
Editorial writing, 77–78
Editors, xvii, 23, 50, 123, 157, 174
    dealing with conflict between, 134–35
    learning from, 7–8, 40–41, 70, 92, 118,
        164–65, 167
    magazine, 158–59
    perfectionist, 126
    women, 135
Education reporter(s), 3, 4–6, 127, 151
Eisenstaedt, Alfred, 173
Elder, Shirley, 58
Elements of Style, The (Strunk and White), xvi,
    40–41
Elston, Wilbur, 77
English language, 75, 76
Epstein, Sid, 57–59, 61
Errors/mistakes, xviii, 119, 141–42
Erwitt, Elliott, 162, 163
Esquire, 81, 86, 154–60
Ethical calls, xvii, 48–49

Fact checking, xvii, 63–70, 154, 162, 163–66
Facts, ix, 112
    getting right, 49–50
    respect for, 23
Feature stories, 69, 140–41
Fettman, Eric, 10
Fineman, Howard, 30
First-year experience, xvii, xvi–xvii, 81
Flint Voice, The, 146, 147
Foren, John, 152

General assignment reporter(s), 62, 115–17
Gerber, Mitch, xvi, 177–81
Gibbs, Tony, 167
Glennon, Frances, xvi, 169–76
Goro, Fritz, 173
Government reporting, 34
    local, 29–30, 31–35, 37–39, 41–42
Graduate degree in journalism, ix, 27, 37, 39,
    45, 51, 150
Graduate school, 27–28
Graves, George, 90
Groer, Anne, xvi, 50–61
Group journalism, 174
Gruber, John, 155
Grunt work, 81, 159

Harper's Bazaar, 86
Hartford Courant, The, 88–94, 126–29
Hines, Bill, 54–55
Hirsch, Dick, 178–79, 180
Hispanics, 102–3
Homicide stories, 48
Hovey, Graham, xv, xviii, 72–80
Human interest stories, 102

Illustration concepts, 135
International News Service, 73–74, 79
Internships, 36, 49, 63, 115, 146–47, 154–55
Interviews, 10, 41, 49, 64, 67–68, 90–91, 98–
    99, 101, 174
    celebrity, 142–43
Investigative reporting, 11, 128
Islands (magazine), 161–68

Jennings, Jim, 29–30
Job search plan(s), 138–40
Johnson, Haynes, 53, 54, 60
Journalism, x, xvi, xxi, 9–10, 28, 175
    as calling, 60, 172
    entry into, xviii–xxi, 22
    as history-in-the-making, 131
    learning by osmosis, 48–49
    reporter and, 25
    writing and, 116
Journalistic personalities, x
Journalistic practices
    questioning, 142, 145
Journalists
    kinds of, 128
    license of, 129–30
Judson, George, xviii, 121–30

Kalikow, Peter, 17
Kaltenbach, Fred, 79
Kastner, Joe, 172
Katz, John, 159
Keefe, Nancy, 44, 45, 49, 50
Kent, Carlton, 55
Kent, Cotton, 55–56, 61
Knight-Ridder News Service, 27

Landers, Ann, 142, 143
Leads, 34, 124, 180–81
    second-day, 3
Learning on the job, 7, 48–49, 51, 54, 69, 70,
    76, 81, 116, 127